Driving Test Skills

Save £40
on your first 10 lessons*
theaa.com/driving-school

AA Driving School

Driving Test Skills

Everything you need to know
to help you pass your Practical Test

Published by AA Publishing (a trading name of AA Media Ltd, whose registered office is Grove House, Chineham Court, Basingstoke, Hampshire RG24 8AG; registered number 06112600).

Information on page 101 reproduced from *The Official Highway Code*. Department for Transport and Driver & Vehicle Standards Agency © Crown Copyright 2022. Reproduced under the terms of the Open Government licence.

Road signs © Crown Copyright 2022. Reproduced under the terms of the Open Government licence.

Part 2 written by Linda Hatswell, Huw Dunley and Keith Bell.
Consultant editors Sue Hubbard, Shaun Thompson, Alan Esam and Keith Bell.
Driving artwork by Chapel Design & Marketing Ltd.

Some sections of this title were previous published as part of the AA's *Practical Test and Driving Skills Manual.*

ISBN: 978-0-7495-8306-4

Printed and bound in the UK by Bell & Bain Ltd.

A05825

CONTENTS

Driving test skills

This book has been written to help you pass your Driving Test. But it is also designed to do more than this, by explaining in detail the skills you need to develop in order to become a safe driver for life.

Each section deals with a specific skill or set of skills that you need to master. You will find references to rules in *The Highway Code*, details of how to do each action or manoeuvre, a practice plan suggesting ways you can help yourself develop that skill or skill set, and a checklist so that you can monitor your own progress. At the end of each section, there are questions for you to work through that will help your understanding of the skill or skill set, with the answers in the following section.

It is important to note that this book does not replace your driving instructor, but is designed to complement your driving lessons and reinforce the skills your instructor has taught you. Use the checklist at the end of each section to monitor your own progress.

The AA also publishes other books that will help you with your Driving Test. *Theory Test* contains all the revision questions and answers from the Driver & Vehicle Standards Agency. *The Highway Code* is essential reading for all drivers and *Know Your Road Signs* provides a clearly illustrated guide to traffic signs and road markings.

Six essential steps to getting your licence

1 GET YOUR PROVISIONAL LICENCE

You can apply online for your provisional licence at www.gov.uk/apply-first-provisional-driving-licence or apply using form D1 available from Post Offices.

The driving licence is issued as a photocard.

You must be at least 17 before you can legally begin learning to drive and you must be in possession of the correct licence documents. Take care when completing all the forms. Many licences cannot be issued for the required date because of errors or omissions on the application. You will need to provide proof of identity, such as a UK passport.

2 LEARN THE HIGHWAY CODE

The Highway Code is essential reading for all drivers and not just those learning to drive. It sets out all the rules for good driving, as well as the rules for other road users such as pedestrians and motorcycle riders. When you have learned the rules you will be able to answer most of the questions in the theory test and be ready to start learning the driving skills you will need to pass your practical test.

Many of these rules contain words in red type. This means that they relate to laws in the Road Traffic Act and other legislation, and therefore MUST be observed.

3 APPLY FOR AND TAKE THE THEORY TEST

The driving test is in two parts, the theory test and the practical test. Once you have a valid provisional licence you may take the theory test at any time, but you must pass it before you are allowed to apply for the practical test. It is important, however, not to take your theory test too early in your course of practical lessons. This is because you need the experience of meeting real hazards, while you are learning to drive, to help you pass the hazard perception element of the theory test.

You can book your theory test online or by phone. You will need your Driver and Vehicle Licensing Agency (DVLA) licence number and your debit or credit card details to hand.

Online: www.gov.uk/book-theory-test
Enquiries and booking support: 0300 200 1122
Welsh speakers: 0300 200 1133
Lines are open Monday to Friday, from 8am to 4pm

4 LEARN TO DRIVE

It is recommended that you learn to drive with an Approved Driving Instructor (ADI). Only an ADI may legally charge for providing tuition. A fully qualified ADI must display a green badge on the windscreen of the car while teaching you. Some trainee driving instructors display a pink badge on the windscreen.

Choose an instructor or driving school by asking friends or relatives for recommendations. Price is important, so find out whether the school offers any discounts for blocks or lessons paid in advance; if you decide to pay in advance, make sure the driving school is reputable. See page 10 for more information.

The most efficient and cost-effective way to learn to drive is to accept that there is no short-cut approach to learning the necessary skills. Agree with your instructor on a planned course of tuition suited to your needs, take regular lessons, and don't skip weeks and expect to pick up where you left off. Ensure the full official syllabus is covered and, as your skills develop, get as much driving practice on the road as possible with a relative or friend. Ensure they are legally able to supervise you; they must be over 21 years of age and have held a full driving licence for at least three years.

5 APPLY FOR AND TAKE THE PRACTICAL TEST

Once you have passed the theory test, and with your instructor's guidance based on your progress, you can plan ahead for a suitable test date for the practical test. You can book your practical test online or by phone.

Online: www.gov.uk/book-driving-test
Enquiries and booking support: 0300 200 1122
Welsh speakers: 0300 200 1133
Lines are open Monday to Friday, from 8am to 12pm

Make sure you have the following details to hand when booking your practical test:

- Theory test pass certificate number
- driver number shown on your licence
- driving school code number (if known)
- your preferred date
- unacceptable days or periods
- if you can accept a test at short notice
- disability or any special circumstances
- your credit/debit card details (the person who books the test must be the cardholder).

If you need to, you can change your practical test appointment online.

Saturday and weekday evening tests are available at some driving test centres. The fee is higher than for a driving test during normal working hours on weekdays. Evening tests are available during the summer months only.

6 APPLY FOR YOUR FULL DRIVING LICENCE

If you have a photocard provisional driving licence issued after 1 March 2004, and pass your driving test, the examiner will send your driving test pass certificate to the DVLA. The DVLA will send your new full licence by post within four weeks of passing your practical test.

If you don't have a photocard provisional driving licence, or you have changed your name, you need to send your Pass Certificate and your provisional licence to the DVLA in Swansea, within two years of passing your practical test.

Getting started

There are several legal requirements you need to satisfy before you get behind the wheel.

DOCUMENTS

- You must hold a provisional licence for the class of vehicle you are driving. You can apply for a provisional licence up to two months before your 17th birthday using form D1 – see page 7 for more details.
- If you are a 16-year-old and hold a 'coming of age' provisional licence for a moped, the entitlement to drive cars is automatically added on your 17th birthday.
- You may not drive on public roads until you are 17 and have received your provisional licence. People with certain disabilities may drive from the age of 16.
- Keep your licence safe. The driving licence is issued by the Driver & Vehicle Licencing Agency as a photocard.

- Any car that you drive must be insured for your use. If driving in your parents' car, they can usually add you to their own insurance simply by phoning their insurer. If you are driving a friend's car, you must be certain that you are covered. Again, a phone call to the insurer will sort this out.
- Any vehicle that you drive must have all the necessary up-to-date paperwork, including valid road tax, an MOT certificate if it is three years old or more, and a Vehicle Registration Certificate.

If stopped by the police or traffic officer you must be able to produce these documents on the spot or within seven days. You may be asked to produce your licence, a certificate of insurance and an MOT certificate. It is a good idea to carry these with you whenever you drive, but don't leave them in the car.

Introduction

VEHICLE

- The car you use to practise in must display red L-plates (or optionally D-plates in Wales) at the front and back. They must be positioned so that they can be clearly seen by other road users and must not obscure your vision in any way. Avoid placing L-plates in the windows – always attach them securely to the body of the car. When you are not driving the car, the L-plates must be removed.
- If using this car for your Driving Test, it must have a proper passenger seat with seatbelt and head restraint fitted. You must also provide a suitable mirror for the examiner's use.

EYESIGHT

- You must be able to read a normal number plate at 20 metres (20m). If you need to wear glasses or contact lenses to do this then you must wear them when driving.

SUPERVISOR

- You are only allowed to drive while accompanied by a qualified driver. They must be over the age of 21 and have held a full driving licence for at least three years.

DRIVING INSTRUCTOR

The best way to learn to drive is to find a fully qualified Approved Driving Instructor (ADI). There will be hundreds listed on the internet, so how can you be sure to find a good one?

- They should be fully qualified and display a green certificate in their windscreen. A pink certificate denotes a trainee instructor. Be careful, as not all trainees ultimately pass their qualifying tests and you will be expected to pay the same as for a fully qualified instructor.
- They should be using a fairly new, well maintained and well presented car. Driving school cars cover extremely high mileages, so any car over two years old is likely to be the equivalent of an eight or nine year old car under normal use. If the instructor drives a dirty or untidy car, what does it tell you about their approach to their business?
- Try to choose an instructor whose car is of medium size. Very small cars are sometimes easy to manoeuvre, but are not ideal if you are going to spend two hours in cramped conditions. It can also be difficult to make the transition from learning in a small car to driving a family saloon. Vehicles such as 4x4s, sports cars, cabriolets or people carriers are not ideal either, as their size makes the manoeuvres much more difficult.
- All ADIs are subject to regular quality control checks conducted by the Driver and Vehicle Standards Agency (DVSA). Failure to achieve a satisfactory standard or not attending these appointments will result in that person's certificate to instruct being withdrawn.
- Consider whether the instructor offers further training, such as Pass Plus courses, motorway training or advanced driver training (see Section 24). Having built up a relationship with your instructor when learning, you may not want to change instructors for post-test training.
- Check with friends or relatives to see if they know of an instructor or company they can recommend.

Make sure any recommendations are for the right reasons. Listen out for words like *thorough, reliable, patient, understanding, calm, challenging, fun, structured, supportive* and so on.

- Price is always a high priority when choosing an instructor, but make sure you consider the value for money. Premium rates should only be applied by fully qualified instructors of a high standard, using modern, well presented vehicles and who are able to offer additional services such as in-car theory tuition, post-test courses, back-up in the event of breakdowns or learning aids such as worksheets. Instructors offering lower rates may not be able to offer such a quality service, or may be relying on low fees to attract pupils because their teaching is not as good as it could be. More often than not, lower fees are a false economy, as you may find that the extra lessons required add up to more than you would otherwise have needed to pay. If the lesson price you are quoted is much lower than others, ask yourself why.
- Be prepared to wait a few weeks to get started with a good instructor – they are likely to be the busiest instructors in your area.
- Ask if the instructor offers discounts for block bookings.

HOW MANY LESSONS?

The number of lessons you will need depends on several factors, not least your ability and determination. DVSA research shows that the average learner takes approximately 45 hours of professional tuition supported by around 22 hours of private practice.

If you are unable to practise outside of lessons, then you are likely to require more hours with an instructor.

The most important factor in this equation is your age. Seventeen year olds will, on average, require fewer lessons than older learners.

When you do arrange lessons, try to book two-hour long sessions. In one-hour lessons, you will spend a significant portion of your time recapping what you learned in your last lesson and travelling to suitable locations. In a two-hour lesson this proportion is much lower – so you can learn much more in one two-hour lesson than in two separate one-hour lessons. This may reduce the number of hours required by up to a third. Make sure you arrange regular lessons – one or more a week is ideal – and maintain continuity of lessons. You cannot expect to start where you left off if you take breaks between lessons.

PRACTICE

Like any other skill, learning to drive can be frustrating, challenging and a chore. Your instructor will make sure that you learn the skills necessary to pass the test and be a safe driver for life, but you don't want to have to pay him or her to practise. The best way to make optimal progress is to ensure that you get plenty of practice between lessons. Do seek advice from your instructor as to when you can begin this supervised practice.

Practice will mean finding someone who is prepared to let you drive them around. Make sure you only practise things you have already covered in lessons – don't try to jump the gun. It is unlikely that your practice car will be fitted with dual controls, so it is essential that you obey any instructions your supervisor gives you, especially the 'Stop' command. Make sure this is the very first thing you do with your supervisor – they need to know you can stop on command.

THE THEORY TEST

Before you are able to book your practical Driving Test you must pass the Theory Test. At the time of writing this consists of 50 multiple choice questions concerning all aspects of driving and a 20-minute Hazard Perception Test containing 14 video clips.

Typically, five of the 50 questions in the multiple choice part of the Theory Test will take the form of a case study. All five questions will be based on a single driving situation and appear one at a time.

Above: Click the mouse when you spot potential hazards – the tractor emerging from the side road (ringed in red).

Case studies are designed to test that you not only know your car theory but also that you understand how to apply your knowledge when faced with a given driving situation.

The case study could be based on any driving scenario and use questions from a range of topics covered by the Theory Test syllabus. The questions are multiple choice and are from the DVSA's databank of unseen Theory Test questions.

A large proportion of the multiple choice questions will be based on the rules in *The Highway Code*, so it is essential that you read and learn everything contained in it. Some questions will relate directly to practical driving skills, making it necessary to study for the Theory Test at the same time as taking driving lessons. You will be given 57 minutes to complete the multiple choice questions.

The computer screen will display the question and an number of possible answers. Using the touch-screen, you select the answer or answers that you think are correct. A useful tip is to decide on your answer before looking at the choices, then select the choice which most closely matches your answer.

Take care to read the question very carefully, and closely examine any diagrams or pictures displayed. Some of the optional answers given may be of similar wording, so take care that your selection means exactly what you intend. You may be asked to provide more than one answer – the question will clearly show how many responses you should mark.

The Hazard Perception Test contains 14 clips from the perspective of a driver. Each clip will contain a developing hazard, except one clip which will contain two developing hazards. You must click the mouse button as soon as you see this developing hazard. Clicking on every hazard you see will not be penalised, unless the programme detects a pattern of clicking that it considers to be cheating. However, only the developing hazard will be scored. Think of your mouse clicks as the equivalent of doing something if you were the driver. As soon as you see a hazard you would check your mirrors, so click once. If that hazard develops and you would need to brake or steer to avoid an accident, click the mouse again.

You must pass both parts of the Theory Test in order to obtain your pass certificate. For the multiple choice questions, the pass mark is 43 out of a possible 50, while for the Hazard Perception Test you must score at least 44 out of 75 to pass.

There are many ways to revise for the Theory Test, and good instructors will suggest facilities to allow you to practise, for example mobile apps, videos, books, theory test papers or lessons structured to teach you hazard perception skills. Make sure that you approach the Theory Test with the same diligence as your practical driving lessons and use your instructor's expertise to help you pass first time.

You responded to this clip in an unacceptable manner. You will score zero for this clip.

Above: You may see a warning screen similar to this one if the computer detects a clicking pattern or you click the mouse constantly.

Remember, to give yourself the best chance of passing your Driving Test first time, you need to take proper and regular lessons with a fully qualified, professional instructor in a modern, reliable car. You should not attempt the test until you are consistently getting it right with your instructor. Take every opportunity to practise privately, but make sure all such practice is conducted legally and in a structured way so that you are only reinforcing the correct skills.

Good luck

AFTER THE PRACTICAL TEST

Drivers may wish to enhance their basic skills and widen their experience by taking further training in the form of the Pass Plus scheme.

This is a six-module syllabus that covers town and rural driving, night driving, driving in adverse weather conditions and driving on dual carriageways and motorways. It offers you the opportunity to gain more driving experience with the help of an instructor. Insurance companies may be prepared to offer discounts to new drivers who have completed the course. There is no test to take at the end of the course. For more details on this scheme, see section 24 – After the Test.

MORE INFORMATION

For more information on learning to drive, including the theory test, the practical test and Pass Plus, visit www.gov.uk/browse/driving.

Part 2: Driving Test Skills and Questions

CONTROLS AND COCKPIT DRILL

You must be familiar with the car's controls: exactly where they are, how and when to use them, and the instructions you may be given in your test relating to their use. You must also know how to set up the car for your use, and make sure it is safe before starting to drive.

How to do it

CONTROLS
Steering wheel
The most prominent control is the steering wheel, which alters the direction of the front wheels of the car.

Think of a clock face. You should hold the wheel at the '10 to 2' position. If you are shorter than average, you may find it more comfortable to hold it in the 'quarter to 3' position.

You should always hold the wheel with both hands, except when one hand is needed for something else, such as changing gear or operating the demisters.

TIP
Always plan to be steering straight ahead when you want to operate other controls such as the radio or windows.

LEGAL REQUIREMENTS
The rules for drivers about the condition of the vehicle and the procedures you need to complete before starting a journey are contained in *The Highway Code*, rules 89–102.

Make small changes of direction by smoothly turning the wheel, keeping your hands in the '10 to 2' position. Your hands should never cross or pass the '6 o'clock' or '12 o'clock' position. When steering further round than this, feed the wheel from hand to hand using the 'pull/push' technique.

The 'pull/push' technique for steering
To steer right, pull the wheel down with your right hand until it reaches the bottom. At the same time, relax the grip of your left hand and slide that hand down so that both hands meet at the bottom. If you need to steer further round, pass the wheel to your left hand and push up, relaxing the grip of your right hand. Again, move both hands together so they meet at the top of the wheel (see diagram, page 18).

Reverse the procedure to straighten up again; don't let the wheel slide through your hands.

Steering right

Steering left

The 'push-pull' technique for steering right: pull the steering wheel down with your right hand, pushing it round with your left hand; then slide your left hand down to meet the right hand at the bottom of the wheel, ready to push it round further if necessary. Reverse the process for steering left.

Stalks

Attached to the steering wheel there are controls on two stalks. The left one usually operates the direction indicator lights and often the headlights as well. To operate the indicators, flick the stalk with outstretched fingers – up for right or down for left. Avoid taking your whole hand off the wheel to signal.

If the stalk also controls the headlights, make sure you know how they work on your car. The commonest method is to twist a 'collar' to turn the lights on, and click the stalk back to switch the main beam on or off. Note that in Japanese-

TIP
If you get confused between left and right signalling, think 'Upright' and 'Let Down'.

built cars the indicators are more usually on the right-hand stalk and the wipers on the left.

The right-hand stalk usually operates the windscreen wipers and washers. Again, make sure you are familiar with the particular details for the car you are driving.

Gear lever

The gear lever is used to select the appropriate gear for the speed you want to drive at. Most modern cars have at least five forward gears and one reverse gear, although smaller and older cars may have just four forward gears.

The forward gears are arranged in an H-shape with fifth gear added at the top right. The central bar of the H is neutral: when the lever is in this position there is no gear selected. The position for reverse varies from model to model, so make sure you know how to select it (for example, you may need to push the lever down to move it to the reverse position).

When you use the gear lever try to be as gentle as possible. Avoid gripping the ball on top. Always aim to keep your hand flat and allow the springs inside the gear mechanism to position the lever for you.

We will explain the details of changing gear in Section 3.

Handbrake

The handbrake keeps the car stationary when parked or stopped. Use the handbrake only when the car is completely still: pulling it on while in motion may cause the brake cable to stretch or snap.

To apply the handbrake, press the button on the end of the lever with your thumb and pull the lever up as far as you can. When you release the button, the lever will lock in position. If you don't use the button you will hear a grating sound. Doing this on a regular basis will wear the ratchet out and eventually it will fail, allowing the car to roll downhill.

To release the handbrake, pull up firmly on the lever and press the button in again.

Push the lever all the way down before you release the button. If the button will not go in, you need to pull the lever up more firmly.

Some cars do not require you to press the button to apply the handbrake – check with your car's manual.

The correct way to hold the gear lever when changing gear

Pedals

Down by your feet you will find three pedals. From right to left these are the Accelerator, Brake and Clutch (ABC).

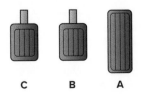

C   B   A

The accelerator, or gas pedal, controls the speed of the engine. Pressing on this pedal will make the engine run faster or 'rev'. You will need to experiment a little to find how much pressure is required. If your car has a rev counter, watch it as you press the pedal. Make sure you don't rev too much (into the red area of the counter) as this can damage the engine. You should keep your heel on the floor and squeeze the pedal by moving your ankle. We will look at this in more detail in the next section.

The footbrake is used to slow or stop the car, or to hold it still for a few seconds. Again, you should try to keep your heel on the floor, and squeeze the pedal smoothly until the car is slowing at the right rate.

Obviously, you will only ever need either the brake or the gas, not both together, so you will only use your right foot for both pedals. When changing from one pedal to the other, use your ankle to swivel your foot. With the engine off, try moving smoothly between the two pedals and pressing each in turn. You must do this without looking down at your feet.

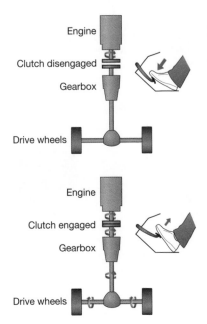

How the clutch works with the engine

The clutch connects the engine to the wheels through the gearbox and is operated by your left foot. There are three positions for the clutch pedal: down, 'biting point' and fully up. We will look at these in more detail in Sections 2 and 3.

When the clutch pedal is down (or de-clutched), the engine is separated from the wheels, so the car can stop while the engine keeps going (see diagram). If the clutch pedal is fully up, the engine and wheels are connected, so anything that the engine does, such as going faster, will be transferred to the wheels.

The point at which the clutch plates touch is called 'biting point'. The exact position of biting point varies from car to car, but is usually about half-way up.

Other controls

There are lots of other controls for you to use. As each car is different, it is impossible to deal with all of them here, but you must know how to operate any control fitted to the car. Make sure you know how the following work:

- lights
- horn
- demisters and heating/ climate controls
- windscreen washers and wipers
- electric doors/central locking
- steering lock/car alarm
- fog lights
- hazard warning lights
- electric windows
- electric door mirrors
- reversing proximity alarm
- parking lights
- variable delay wipers and rear wipers
- sun roof
- boot/bonnet/petrol cap release

THE DRIVER'S COCKPIT: BASICS

1 handbrake
2 clutch pedal
3 brake pedal
4 accelerator/ gas pedal
5 ignition switch/ steering lock
6 lighting switch
7 windscreen wiper and washer
8 side mirror
9 instruments and warning lights
10 rear-view mirror
11 direction indicators and horn
12 fog lights
13 gear change lever

You must also be familiar with the instrument panel and warning lights. After you have started the engine, the warning lights will come on only if there is a problem. If any warning lights show while you are driving, it is important that you stop and check. You could cause serious damage to the car or even cause an accident if you proceed. Your car's manual should give full details – keep it in the glovebox for easy reference.

COCKPIT DRILL

Before you start the engine, you must adjust various settings of the car to suit you and make sure that the vehicle is safe. This is known as the 'cockpit drill'.

Doors

Check that all the doors, as well as the bonnet and boot, are properly closed. Listen for a solid 'thunk' and, if there is a relevant warning lamp, check the instrument panel. If you can hear a deep rattling sound, it may be that a door is not closed properly.

Before you start the engine you must ensure that you are sitting correctly and comfortably in the driving seat: check your distance from the pedals and the steering wheel, your height, the angle of the back of the seat and the position of the head restraint

Seat

Adjust the position of the seat to suit you, so that you can comfortably reach all the controls. There are usually four adjustments you can make.

* Distance from the pedals: move the seat forward or back so that your left foot can fully depress the clutch without stretching.
* Seat height: you should be as high as necessary in the seat to give you the best view of the road ahead. Make sure the seat height doesn't prevent you reaching the pedals or cause your head to touch the roof.
* Backrest rake: angle the back of the seat so that you are comfortably upright.
* Head restraint: the centre of the restraint should be about level with your eyes. This will help prevent neck injuries in the event of a crash.

Steering

* The steering wheel may be adjustable. If so, adjust it so that when holding the wheel at the '12 o'clock' position, your elbows are slightly bent. Make sure the wheel doesn't obscure any part of the speedometer.

Seatbelt

Put on your seatbelt. Make sure the belt is not twisted. Pull up the strap across your chest so that the lap belt is firmly against your body and over the hips – a slack belt can not only cause pelvic or chest injuries in case of an accident, but also allows your upper body to move further than it should.

TIP

If the seatbelt anchor point by your shoulder is adjustable, make sure it is 2–3cm higher than your shoulder.

Remember, you are responsible for ensuring that any passenger under the age of 14 is wearing a seatbelt. If they are over the age of 14, it is their own responsibility, but you should remind them if necessary. Rule 100 in *The Highway Code* gives details of the requirements for children under the age of 14.

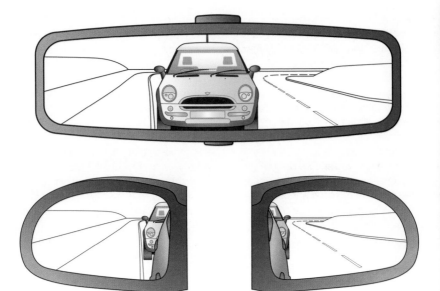

The correct adjustments – make sure you can see as much as possible of the road behind in your three mirrors

Mirrors

Adjust the mirrors so that you get the best possible view behind you (see above). Try to sit normally as you move the mirrors – if you lean over you will change your angle of view.

Adjust the interior rear-view mirror so that you can see the top of the rear window at the top edge of the mirror. Try to adjust it so that you can see both top corners of the window and a little of your head restraint.

In the door mirrors you should be able to see a little of the side of the car. The horizon line should be across the centre of the mirror.

Having adjusted your mirrors, move around in your seat to make sure you are comfortable, and then check the mirrors again.

In summary then, the cockpit drill consists of:
- doors
- seat
- steering
- seatbelt
- mirrors.

Finally, before starting the engine you must make sure the car is secure. Pull up the handbrake to make sure it is fully on, and check that the gear lever is in neutral by pushing against the spring.

You are now ready to start the engine.

You should perform these adjustments and checks every time you get into the car, even if you were the last person to drive the vehicle. A pedestrian may have knocked your mirrors, or a passenger accidentally knocked the gear lever into a different position. You may find that you need to adjust your mirrors later the same day as your body slowly sinks in the seat, or the day's work causes you to slump more.

Practice plan

Make sure you use the cockpit drill every time you get in the driver's seat, and always check the car is secure before starting the engine.

As you progress through your lessons, you will find you need to use new controls. Make sure you know where to find them in every car you drive and how to operate them.

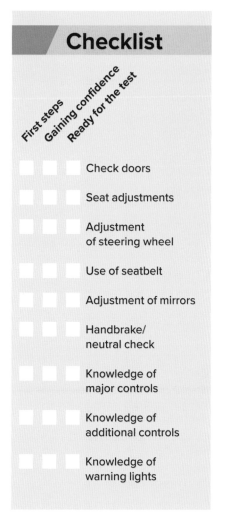

Checklist

First steps · Gaining confidence · Ready for the test

- Check doors
- Seat adjustments
- Adjustment of steering wheel
- Use of seatbelt
- Adjustment of mirrors
- Handbrake/ neutral check
- Knowledge of major controls
- Knowledge of additional controls
- Knowledge of warning lights

1

To use the controls safely you need to adopt a suitable driving position. There are a number of checks you should make.

Fill in the missing words

1 Check the h _ _ _ _ _ _ _ _ is on.

2 Check the d _ _ _ _ are shut.

3 Check your s _ _ _ is in the correct position.

4 Check the h _ _ _
r _ _ _ _ _ _ _ _ is adjusted to give maximum protection.

5 Check the driving m _ _ _ _ _ _ are adjusted to give maximum rear view.

6 Check your s _ _ _ b _ _ _ is securely fastened.

2

Which foot should you use for each of these controls (in cars with a manual gearbox)?

R = Right foot   **L** = Left foot
The foot-brake ☐
The clutch ☐
The accelerator ☐

3

Here is a list of functions and a list of controls.

Match each function to its control by placing the appropriate letter in the box

THE FUNCTIONS	THE CONTROLS
A To control the direction in which you want to travel	☐ The handbrake
B To slow or stop the vehicle	☐ The driving mirrors
C To increase or decrease the engine's speed	☐ The gear lever
D To give you a clear view behind	☐ The clutch
E To hold the vehicle still when it is stationary	☐ The steering wheel
F To enable you to change gear	☐ The foot-brake
G To enable you to make or break contact between the engine and the wheels	☐ The accelerator

---

4

The accelerator can also be called the g _ _ pedal

Fill in the missing word

5

Are the following statements about steering true or false?

Tick the appropriate boxes

	True	False
1 I must keep both hands on the wheel at all times.	☐	☐
2 To keep good control I should feed the wheel through my hands.	☐	☐
3 I can place my hands at any position as long as I am comfortable.	☐	☐
4 When going round corners, it is best to cross my hands (hand over hand).	☐	☐
5 I should never take both hands off the wheel when the vehicle is moving.	☐	☐
6 To straighten up I should feed the wheel back through my hands.	☐	☐

6

The steering lock is...

A The locking mechanism that stops the steering wheel from moving when the ignition key is removed

B The angle through which the wheels turn when the steering wheel is turned

Answer ☐

7

Match each of the following functions to its control.

THE FUNCTIONS	THE CONTROLS
A To enable you to see the road ahead and other road users to see you without causing dazzle	☐ The direction indicators
B To show other road users which way you intend to turn	☐ Dipped beam
C To use only when visibility is 100 metres/yards or less	☐ Main beam
D To enable you to see further, but not to be used when there is oncoming traffic	☐ Rear fog lamp
E To warn other road users of your presence	☐ Horn
F To warn other road users when you are temporarily obstructing traffic	☐ Hazard lights

MOVING OFF AND STOPPING NORMALLY

You must be able to move away safely, under full control, and take up the proper position in the road. You must also select and stop in a safe position, close and parallel to the kerb.

How to do it

MOVING OFF
Check the handbrake is applied and the gear leaver is in neutral before you start the engine.

The routine to use now is **POM**:
Preparation
Observation
Manoeuvre

Preparation
Prepare the car by pressing the clutch down and selecting first gear. Keep hold of the top of the steering wheel with your right hand, and hold the handbrake ready to release it with your left.

With your right foot, set some gas (press on the accelerator pedal). You want to hear the engine humming clearly. If your car has a rev counter, set the revs to about double the tick-over speed (tick-over speed is the number of revs the engine settles to when your foot is completely off the gas pedal). Try resting your foot on the gas pedal and simply curling your toes. On some cars, this will bring the revs up just enough to move the vehicle forward on a flat road.

> **TIP**
> Remember to keep your hand flat when you use the gear lever and use your palm – don't curl your fingers over the gear knob.

LEGAL REQUIREMENTS
Rules 159–161 of *The Highway Code* deal with moving off, and the checks you should make first. Rules 238–252 deal with waiting and parking, including parking restrictions, safety, and parking on a hill.

Slowly bring the clutch pedal (left foot) up to biting point. Try to keep your heel on the floor if you can, as you will get used to the feeling of your shin muscles tightening. You should feel a slight tug or notice the bonnet rise a fraction as you reach biting point, and the revs will drop. Keep enough gas on to prevent the engine from stalling. Keep your feet still.

Observation
Look systematically all around the car. Start on your left and work your way through every window and mirror in turn to look over your right shoulder. You are looking for anything that is moving or that could prevent you from moving off safely, such as pedestrians, other vehicles or animals. Wait until you are sure it is safe to move. The most important observation is the area to the right and rear of the car that is not picked up in the mirrors. This is a 'blind spot', and you must not move until you are sure it is clear. Signal if necessary.

Manoeuvre

If it is safe to move off, release the handbrake and keep your feet still. The car will move forward slowly. Let it move about half a car's length before you gently squeeze the gas pedal down and at the same time smoothly bring the clutch up all the way. We will refer to this movement as 'pedalling'.

As you move forwards, steer very gently to the right until the left side of the car is about 1m from the left kerb. Turn the steering wheel the same amount to the left to straighten the car in the road before turning the wheel back to its straight position.

Press the clutch down

Select first gear

Set some gas

Raise clutch to biting point

TIP

You should always keep well to the left side of the road, normally about 1m from the kerb. If the road is too narrow to allow this, then slow down.

Make all-round observation

Check blind spot

Release the handbrake

Release clutch slowly, gently squeeze gas

Above: the correct sequence for moving off

Stopping

The routine used to stop the car is the most important routine you will learn. You'll use it for nearly everything you do when you are driving – not just stopping. Ask yourself: Is it **Safe**? Is it **Legal**? Is it **Convenient**?

Mirrors–signal–manoeuvre

Position–speed–look

Usually abbreviated to **MSM** or **MSM/PSL**, this routine is often called the 'hazard routine'. This makes sense if you consider that a manoeuvre can be defined as **any change of speed or direction** and a hazard is **anything which may make you change speed or direction**.

MSM tells you that you must always check your mirrors and consider giving a signal before changing speed or direction.

PSL reminds you that you must position your vehicle correctly before slowing (or occasionally accelerating) to the correct speed and selecting the appropriate gear. Then look to check if it is still safe to carry out the manoeuvre.

It is vital that you follow the MSM/PSL sequence in full, even if, on some occasions, you do not actually do anything. If you find you are unable to complete the sequence, then you are almost certainly going too fast.

When you are stopping, the routine works like this. First, you will need to spot where you intend to stop on your own (left) side of the road. Find a place where you will not cause problems for other road users or break any parking restrictions.

Having found your chosen spot:

Mirrors – Check the main mirror, as you will be slowing down, and check your left mirror, as you will be moving over to the left. If there is anything behind or around you, you will need to...

Signal – Let other road users know what you intend to do. Consider signalling left to warn any other road user that you are about to slow down or turn left. There is no need to signal if there is nobody around to see it.

Manoeuvre – To change the speed and direction of the car, split the manoeuvre into three further stages:

Position – If it is safe, steer gently towards the kerb and at the same time...

Speed – Take your foot off the gas pedal and move it to the footbrake. Gently squeeze the brake until the car is slowing down enough.

Look – Look in your left door mirror to check you are close enough to the kerb.

When you are about one car length from where you want to stop, push the clutch pedal all the way down.

Keep a steady pressure on the footbrake until the last 10cm before you stop. At this point ease off the brake very slightly – just a couple of millimetres up should do – so that the car stops smoothly. Keep your feet still, pressing down on both brake and clutch pedals.

As soon as the car has stopped completely, apply the handbrake and move the gear lever back into neutral. You can now safely take your feet off the pedals.

If you had indicated to show you were stopping, cancel the signal.

> **TIP**
> Always put the handbrake on before you select neutral. This will stop the car from moving too much if your foot slips off the clutch.

Practice plan

First steps
Find a long, straight section of road or an empty car park to practise on.

Next, with the engine on, practise setting the gas to the right level. Remember to listen to the engine.

Now practise finding the biting point with the clutch pedal. Each time you find it, hold your foot still for a few seconds before pushing the pedal down to the floor again. In between tries, return to neutral and take both feet off the pedals. If you hold biting point for too long you will wear the clutch mechanism out very quickly.

Finally, practise moving away smoothly. Remember to keep your feet still as you release the handbrake.

Gaining confidence
Practise the moving off routine on a quiet road. Work on timing the routine so that you are ready to go just as you are sure that it is safe. Avoid holding biting point for more than a few seconds. Make sure that you develop the habit of checking your blind spots.

Concentrate on steering to the correct position in the road.

Obviously, you will also practise stopping. Try to stop as close as possible to your chosen spot. Practise stopping exactly alongside selected lampposts or drainage grids. Be careful not to scrape the tyres on the kerb, and make sure you stop with your steering wheel straight.

Ready for the test

Practise moving off and stopping in busy traffic. Make sure you always use the MSM/PSL routine properly.

Practise stopping smoothly, without any bumps or jerks: remember to ease off the brake pedal slightly as you come to a halt.

TIP

In your driving test, you will be expected to show that you can control the car smoothly. If you should stall, put the gears in neutral and the handbrake on, and start again.

Checklist

First steps	Gaining confidence	Ready for the test	
☐	☐	☐	Routine before starting engine
☐	☐	☐	Hand position on gear lever
☐	☐	☐	Use of accelerator pedal
☐	☐	☐	Use of clutch
☐	☐	☐	Observations, especially blind spots
☐	☐	☐	Use of handbrake
☐	☐	☐	Accuracy of steering
☐	☐	☐	Road position
☐	☐	☐	Use of footbrake
☐	☐	☐	Use of MSM/PSL

1

**The following is a list of actions involved in moving off from rest.
Number the boxes 1 to 9 to show the correct sequence**

The first box has been filled in to give you a start

1 **A** Press the clutch down fully

☐ **B** Check your mirrors

☐ **C** Set the accelerator pedal

☐ **D** Move the gear lever into 1st gear

☐ **E** Decide whether you need
to give a signal

☐ **F** Let the clutch come to biting point
and hold it steady

☐ **G** Check your blind spot

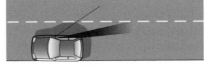

☐ **H** If safe, release the handbrake and let
the clutch up a little more

☐ **I** Press the accelerator pedal a little
more and let the clutch up fully

2

The following is a list of actions required for stopping normally.
Number the boxes 1 to 9 to show the correct sequence.

The first box has been filled in to give you a start

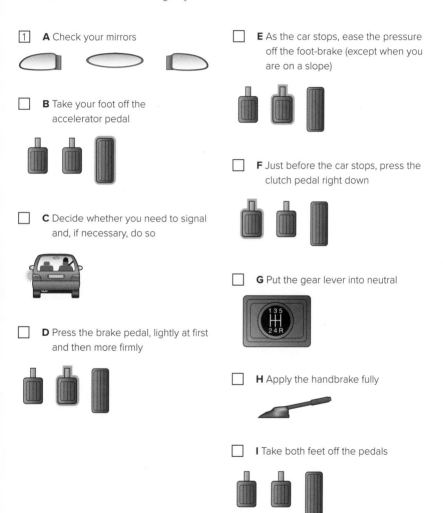

[1] **A** Check your mirrors

[ ] **B** Take your foot off the accelerator pedal

[ ] **C** Decide whether you need to signal and, if necessary, do so

[ ] **D** Press the brake pedal, lightly at first and then more firmly

[ ] **E** As the car stops, ease the pressure off the foot-brake (except when you are on a slope)

[ ] **F** Just before the car stops, press the clutch pedal right down

[ ] **G** Put the gear lever into neutral

[ ] **H** Apply the handbrake fully

[ ] **I** Take both feet off the pedals

CLUTCH CONTROL AND CHANGING GEAR

You must use the clutch pedal to control the speed of the car when moving at very slow speeds, for example when manoeuvring or in slow-moving queues of traffic. You must use the correct gear for the speed you are travelling, changing gear smoothly and without looking down or steering erratically.

How to do it

CLUTCH CONTROL

Clutch control is all about keeping the car moving at a very slow speed – the sort of thing you will need to do when queuing or manoeuvring the car in a limited space.

The clutch is the mechanism that connects the engine to the wheels. As we mentioned in Section 1, there are three positions. With the pedal all the way down, the clutch plates separate and no engine power is transmitted to the wheels. When the pedal is all the way up, the engine connects directly to the wheels (see below).

The most important position is 'biting point' – the position where the two clutch plates just touch lightly. At this point, the engine tries to make the wheels turn but the action of the handbrake or footbrake prevents the car from moving. Because the handbrake only operates on the rear wheels, the front of the car can move very slightly as the suspension takes up

LEGAL REQUIREMENTS
The only reference to the use of the clutch or gears in *The Highway Code* is rule 122. This rule concerns coasting – that is, travelling with the clutch down or in neutral. You must NEVER coast as it reduces your control of the vehicle.

the slack, so at biting point, you can expect the nose of the car to rise slightly. Listen and you will also notice the revs drop as some of the power is used in trying to move the car.

To move away very slowly, select first gear and follow the procedure for a normal move away, but without bringing the clutch pedal up too high. Set enough gas so that the engine makes a steady hum, about double the idling speed.

How the clutch engages the engine

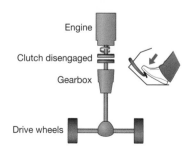

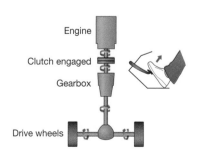

Now slowly bring the clutch up until you notice the nose of the car rising slightly and the revs drop a fraction. At this point, you must keep your feet still. Make sure it is safe to move off by making all-round observations and check the blind spot. The instant you release the handbrake, the car should move slowly forward.

As soon as you reach the speed you want, dip the clutch slightly by pressing the pedal down one or two millimetres. The car should gradually slow down. To maintain the same speed, bring the clutch pedal back up to biting point, again just a couple of millimetres. By 'feathering' the clutch pedal like this, you can keep the car moving very slowly without stopping.

If you do need to stop, you can keep the clutch pedal at biting point as you use the footbrake to come gently to a halt. This has the same effect as finding the biting point with the handbrake on; you are instantly ready to go.

> **TIP**
> Your left foot should rest on the floor to the left of the pedal except when you are using the clutch.

Holding the clutch at biting point causes much more wear and tear on the clutch than having it either fully up or down. You should not hold biting point any longer than is absolutely necessary. For example, if you have seen a traffic light turn red and have stopped, you should normally wait in neutral until the red and

amber lights show, only then setting your gas and finding biting point. With practice, you will be able to do this very quickly.

CHANGING GEAR

Changing gear smoothly and at the right time is a skill that not only makes your driving smooth and comfortable, but also greatly reduces the wear and tear on the car and improves fuel consumption.

To change gear smoothly, you first need to decide when to change. Try to avoid changing gear when you are steering or braking; you should select the correct gear before turning and after you have braked to the speed you want.

If you are accelerating, you should listen to the engine noise or glance at the rev counter. Under normal driving conditions you would probably change up a gear when the revs reach about half the maximum. At this level, the engine noise will be very noticeable, but not overpowering. Of course, if you are

SPEEDS FOR EACH GEAR

Gear	Speed range	Changing up at
1st	0–18mph	As soon as possible
2nd	5–30mph	20mph
3rd	15–50mph	30mph
4th	28–70mph	40mph or when cruising
5th	35–70mph	

travelling uphill or in the process of overtaking, you will need the extra power a lower gear gives you. In such cases you may let the revs go beyond this half-way point, but take care not to allow excessive revving.

As a guide, the table on the previous page shows the approximate range of speeds for each gear and the speed at which you should normally change up. As you experience driving in different cars you'll discover that different makes and models have their own specific gearing ranges, and you should take advice from the manual for that car or its manufacturer.

Having decided to change gear, establish that you're going fast enough to change into the higher gear. Now take your right foot off the gas pedal and then depress the clutch with your left foot. Move your left hand from the steering wheel to the gear lever. Remember to keep your hand flat and use your palm – do not grip the knob.

As soon as the clutch pedal is completely down, select the new gear, keeping your hand flat and using only gentle pressure on the gear lever. As soon as you have selected the gear, bring the clutch up slowly to the top of its travel before smoothly and progressively pressing down on the gas pedal. Return your left hand to the steering wheel and your left foot to its resting position.

TIP
To bring the clutch up slowly, try saying out loud 'Bring the clutch up slowly,' as you move your foot. It should take you that long to move the pedal all the way from the bottom to the top.

As you change gear, keep your eyes on the road ahead and be conscious of steering accurately with your right hand. If you find your steering drifts as you change gears, stiffen your right arm slightly by pushing gently forward on the steering wheel.

Changing down
When changing down to a lower gear the process is almost the same, the only small difference being that you may need to apply very gentle pressure on the gas pedal as you bring the clutch back up. This brings the engine speed back up closer to the speed of the wheels and gets rid of the slight bump you may feel as the clutch comes up.

Block changes, up as well as down
There is no need to change through each gear in turn when speeding up or slowing down. Modern cars are able to change from fifth to first gear directly. It is acceptable to make block changes, e.g., fourth to second, as there is less time spent with the clutch down and steering with one hand.

If you are travelling at 50mph approaching a left turn, for example, the correct sequence should be:

Mirrors – main and left

Signal – left

Position – normal road position, 1m from the kerb

Speed – brake smoothly and progressively to about 10–15mph, off brake, change gear from fifth to second

Look – into side road and left mirror again; also look for pedestrians on the pavement

Make the turn

Check mirrors and accelerate away smoothly.

> **TIP**
> Remember, the rule is BBC – Brake Before Clutch. Slow down to the speed you want and only then declutch and change gear.

With practice, you will find that there are times when changing up through the gears, that skipping a gear is appropriate and acceptable. For example, on the open road, when reaching higher speeds, moving from third gear to fifth gear is fine.

In summary then, to change gear:
- move your left hand to the gear lever
- foot off gas
- clutch down
- select new gear
- bring clutch up slowly
- foot on gas
- left hand back to steering wheel, left foot to resting position.

Practice plan

First steps
With the engine switched off, practise changing through the gears without looking down. Follow the sequence given opposite as if you were moving, saying each stage out loud as you do it.

Turn the engine off. Practise bringing the clutch pedal up slowly in the time it takes to say 'Bring the clutch up slowly'.

On a quiet road, practise moving off and changing up through the gears. Get to about 25–30mph and then slow down again to around 10mph. At this speed, change back down into second gear before accelerating and changing up again.

Practise moving as slowly as possible using clutch control.

Gaining confidence

Find a road with busy, queuing traffic. Practise clutch control in the queue. Try to maintain a good gap in front of you so that you can keep moving slowly, rather than driving in a 'stop-start' manner.

On faster roads, practise changing up through the gears as you accelerate, using fifth gear if possible. Remember to use block changes when appropriate, and when slowing down take care to brake to the speed you want before changing gear.

Ready for the test

On roads where the national speed limit applies, practise changing up and down through the gears. Make sure you are always in the appropriate gear for the speed you are doing and for the road and traffic conditions. Remember to use lower gears for more power or engine braking, and the higher gears for economy and smoothness.

Try to find some steep hills on which to practise gear changes. When going down a hill, use a lower gear for the engine braking it provides. When going up a hill, use a lower gear to give you more power. Try to select the lower gear well before it becomes necessary; remember you will slow down quite dramatically when changing gear as you go uphill.

Checklist

First steps *Gaining confidence* *Ready for the test*

- Clutch control
- Changing gear at the correct moment
- Using the appropriate gear for the speed

Sequence

- Clutch down
- Off gas
- Hand down to lever
- Select gear
- Clutch up slowly
- On gas
- Left hand and foot return
- Hand position on lever
- Block changes up/down
- Gear selection for hills

1

Which gear gives you the most power?

Answer ☐

2

Number the boxes to show the correct sequence of actions required when changing up.

The first box has been filled in for you

- [1] **A** Place your left hand on the gear lever
- ☐ **B** Move the gear lever to the next highest position
- ☐ **C** Press the clutch pedal down fully and ease off the accelerator pedal
- ☐ **D** Let the clutch pedal come up fully and, at the same time, press the accelerator pedal
- ☐ **E** Put your left hand back on the steering wheel

3

If you were travelling at 60mph on a clear road, which gear would you most likely select?

Answer ☐

4

Are the following statements about changing down true or false?

Tick the appropriate boxes **True** **False**

1 I would stay in the highest ☐ ☐ gear as long as possible, even if my engine started to labour

2 I would change down early ☐ ☐ so that the engine helps to slow the car down

3 I would avoid using the ☐ ☐ foot-brake as much as possible

4 I would usually slow the car ☐ ☐ down by using the foot-brake first. Then, when I am at the required speed, I would change down to the appropriate gear

5 I would always change down ☐ ☐ through the gears so that I do not miss out any intermediate gears

5

When changing gear, I should look...

1 Ahead ☐

2 At the gear lever ☐

3 At my feet ☐

Which is correct?

6
Do's and don'ts

Tick the appropriate boxes   **Do**   **Don't**

1 Force the gear lever if there is any resistance ☐ ☐

2 Rush the gear changes ☐ ☐

3 Match your speed with the correct gear ☐ ☐

4 Use the brakes, where necessary, to reduce speed before changing down ☐ ☐

5 Listen to the sound of the engine ☐ ☐

6 Take your eyes off the road when changing gear ☐ ☐

7 Hold the gear lever longer than necessary ☐ ☐

8 Coast with the clutch down or the gear lever in neutral ☐ ☐

7
Pushing the clutch pedal down...

A Releases the engine from the wheels
B Engages the engine with the wheels

Answer ☐

8
The point where the clutch plates meet is called the b_ _ _ _ _ point.

Fill in the missing word

9
By controlling the amount of contact between the clutch plates, it is possible to control the speed of the car.

Would you use this control...

Tick the appropriate boxes   **YES**   **NO**

1 When moving away from rest? ☐ ☐

2 When manoeuvring the car in reverse gear? ☐ ☐

3 When slowing down to turn a corner? ☐ ☐

4 In very slow moving traffic? ☐ ☐

5 To slow the car down? ☐ ☐

10
You need to change gear to match your e_ _ _ _ _ speed to the speed at which your v_ _ _ _ _ _ is travelling. The s_ _ _ _ _ the engine is making will help you know w_ _ _ to change gear.

Complete the sentences

TURNING LEFT AND RIGHT

You must be able to turn from a major road into a minor road safely and under full control. You will need to use the MSM/PSL routine to ensure that other road users understand your intentions. You will also need to make sure you corner at a suitable speed, using the correct gear.

How to do it

Use the MSM/PSL routine to guide you through the manoeuvre. Start the routine as soon as you see a sign for a junction ahead, or as soon as you see the junction itself. As you approach the junction, look ahead for gaps between buildings or parked cars – these can give you clues about where the side road might be.

MIRRORS

Check your main mirror and the door mirror in the direction you intend to turn. If there is anything following you too closely, you may need to give an earlier signal to encourage them to drop back before you slow down. You are also looking for drivers attempting to overtake on either side. If there is a vehicle about to overtake your car, you should have time to let it pass before you indicate. Remember, you are checking your mirrors to see whether it is safe to signal.

TIP
If your mirrors show that there is a vehicle following too closely, brake very gently so that you only light up the brake lights – to encourage the other driver to drop back. This is called 'braking for two'.

LEGAL REQUIREMENTS
The Highway Code rules 179–183 deal with turning at junctions.

SIGNAL
If it is safe, indicate to show other road users that you intend to turn. If there are several possible turnings, make sure your signal cannot be misunderstood by others – delay your indicators if necessary, and use your brake lights to show that you are slowing down.

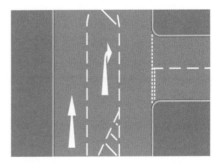

If you intend to turn right you should move as close to the centre line as possible, or into the right-hand lane if there is one. Some right-hand turns will have a separate area marked on the road surface for you to wait in. Use these areas to allow following traffic to pass on your left.

SPEED

You now need to slow down to take the turn safely. For a left turn, you should judge your speed on what you can see around the corner. You should go no faster than 1mph for every 1m you can see along your route (see also Section 7). For a tight corner this could mean going as slowly as 5mph, while you might be able to take a sweeping corner at 15mph or more. It is obviously better to go slower rather than faster at first. With practice you will get better at judging the best speed to use.

For right turns you will probably need to slow down more, as most are 90-degree turns that make it difficult to see into the new road until you are almost at your turning point. You will also be crossing the path of oncoming traffic, so it is more likely that you may have to stop. As a general rule, slow down to a fast walking speed for right turns, about 5 or 6mph, and always be prepared to stop.

Don't forget that the vehicle following you may not expect you to slow down quite as much as you do: brake smoothly and progressively so that they get plenty of warning.

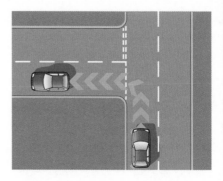

This shows the correct position in the road for turning left

When you have reached the desired speed you should still be two or three car lengths from the turn. This allows you time to change into the appropriate gear for the speed you are now doing. For left turns, this will usually be second gear. For right turns you may be able to see enough to use second gear, but always be prepared to stop and select first if necessary.

If you do have to stop and wait, make sure you stop at the turning point. That will be when your front wheels are level with the centre line of the road into which you intend to turn. On most cars you should see the centre line of the new road level with the bottom edge of your door mirror.

TIP

To avoid doing more than one thing at a time, make sure you brake to the speed you need before you change gear.

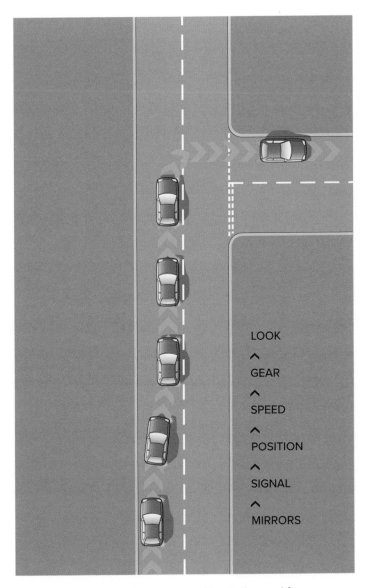

LOOK

^

GEAR

^

SPEED

^

POSITION

^

SIGNAL

^

MIRRORS

This illustration shows the correct position in the road for turning right

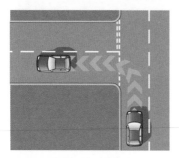

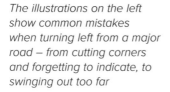

The illustrations on the left show common mistakes when turning left from a major road – from cutting corners and forgetting to indicate, to swinging out too far

The illustrations on the right show common mistakes when turning right, from starting from the wrong position on the road, to cutting the corner and 'swan-necking'

'Swan-necking' happens when turning right into a minor road. It is caused by steering once you have passed the centre lines, which is too late. This creates a 'swan neck' effect (see illustration). If you turn too late, you could hit the kerb or the car behind you might think you have decided not to turn.

TIP
As you turn, use a little pressure on the gas to maintain a steady speed, but don't accelerate until you are travelling straight again.

LOOK

As a pedestrian, you are already able to judge a safe gap to cross the road. You are likely to drive across faster than you would walk, so you could use this 'pedestrian gap' as a measure of a safe gap. If you would walk across in front of an oncoming vehicle you should be able to drive across safely.

You now need to look into the road you intend to take. You are checking for obstructions which may prevent you from turning. Always give way to pedestrians in the road: stop at the turning point, if necessary, to let them cross.

Check your door mirror to be sure no one is attempting to pass. If you're turning right, someone could be about to overtake, or, if turning left, a cyclist may be about to pass on your left, especially if the traffic is moving slowly.

As you turn, make sure you position yourself correctly. When you are turning left, you should keep your normal road position – 1m from the kerb. If turning right, you must take care not to cut the corner. Imagine a policeman is standing where the 'Give Way' and centre lines meet; you must not run over his toes, or pass on the wrong side of him. Keep the T formed by these lines in your door window as you turn. As you straighten out check your position again and look in your mirrors to see if anything has followed you in. If your indicator has not cancelled itself automatically, turn it off manually.

Practice plan

First steps
On a quiet 30mph road, time how long it takes you to turn right from stationary. This will probably be around 3 or 4 seconds. Now drive along the same road without turning right. Start counting as you pass the junction and see how far down the road you are after 5 or 6 seconds. At this point, try to spot a marker of some sort, such as a lamppost or grid. Drive the same route and try again, this time starting to count as you pass the marker. Make sure you are driving at an appropriate speed. In this way you can judge how far from the turning another car could be before it would be safe for you to make your original right turn.

Now that you have a way of judging a safe gap, practise taking right turns on busier roads. Make sure that you have plenty of practice, both of clear junctions and also those where you have to stop.

Practise left turns as well, saying the MSM/PSL routine out loud as you do them.

Gaining confidence
Practise turning left and right on busier roads, including right turns that have yellow boxes (see page 114) or from separate right-turn lanes. Find some turns with traffic lights to practise on, especially those with filter lights.

Concentrate at first on getting the speed and gear right, then shift your emphasis to positioning.

Ready for the test

Next, practise on very busy roads, concentrating on getting your timing right. Try to approach right turns at such a speed that you do not have to stop completely.

Include junctions with lanes, yellow box markings, filter arrows, roads at acute angles (very sharp turns, almost doubling back on yourself) and Y-junctions.

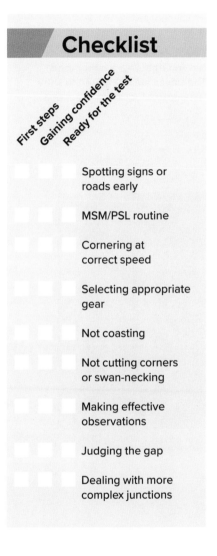

Checklist

First steps	Gaining confidence	Ready for the test	
☐	☐	☐	Spotting signs or roads early
☐	☐	☐	MSM/PSL routine
☐	☐	☐	Cornering at correct speed
☐	☐	☐	Selecting appropriate gear
☐	☐	☐	Not coasting
☐	☐	☐	Not cutting corners or swan-necking
☐	☐	☐	Making effective observations
☐	☐	☐	Judging the gap
☐	☐	☐	Dealing with more complex junctions

1

The diagram below shows a car turning right into a minor road. The boxes are numbered to show the correct sequence of actions.

Complete the sentence:

At point 5 you should look and

a _ _ _ _ _ the situation,

d _ _ _ _ _ to go or wait,

and a _ _ accordingly.

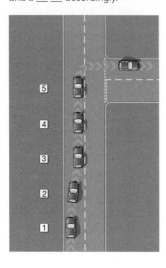

2

When turning left into a minor road, which diagram below shows the best path to follow?

Answer ☐

3

You turn into a side road. Pedestrians are already crossing it. Should you...

Tick the appropriate box:

A Sound your horn ☐

B Slow down and give way ☐

C Flash your lights ☐

D Wave them across ☐

4

When approaching and turning left into a minor road, as shown in the diagram, which gear would you most likely use?

Answer ☐

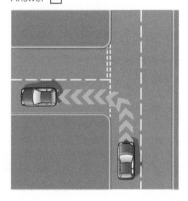

5

When turning right into a minor road, which diagram shows the best path to follow?

Answer ☐

EMERGING LEFT AND RIGHT

You must be able to emerge at a T-junction (turn from a minor road onto a major road) safely and with due regard for other road users. You need to know how to assess the junction as 'open' or 'closed' and how to apply the MSM/PSL routine in each case. You must also know the meanings of the road markings and signs, especially the difference between 'Stop' and 'Give Way'. For information on dealing with traffic lights at junctions, see Section 10.

How to do it

The MSM/PSL routine will help you to negotiate T-junctions safely. Start the routine as soon as you can see a sign for the junction ahead or the junction itself. Your instructor will usually say 'At the end of the road, turn...'

Mirrors

As soon as you hear the instruction, or you see the junction, check your main mirror and the door mirror in the direction you intend to turn. Check to see if there is anything following too closely or attempting to overtake you – just as you learned for left and right turns.

Signal

As a guide give a signal as soon as you can read the Give Way or Stop sign. There is always the possibility that there is a turning off into a side road before you reach the end of the road, so you must check before you indicate. If you can't see to the end of the road, you can delay using your indicators, as your brake lights will tell the driver behind you that you are slowing down.

Position

If you intend to turn left, maintain your normal road position 1m from the kerb. If you intend to turn right, move over to a position as close to the centre line as is safe, remembering that traffic turning into your road from the main road ahead may swing out across the line.

LEGAL REQUIREMENTS
The Highway Code deals with junctions in rules 170–178. The law is clear about the rules for stopping at junctions – check rules 171 and 172. Rules 175–178 deal with what to do at junctions with traffic lights.

Speed

Now you need to assess the junction. You must decide whether the junction is 'open', 'closed' or 'blind'.

- An open junction is one where you can see clearly that it is safe to emerge without stopping. You need to be able to see clearly that there is a safe gap in the traffic on both sides of the junction, and that the junction is a 'Give Way'. Don't forget to check the pavements as well – you must give way to any pedestrians in the road.
- A closed junction is one where you cannot see clearly to one or both sides, or you can see that you will have to give way.
- A blind junction is one where you still cannot see clearly even when you are at the line and you will definitely have to stop. Obviously, every Stop sign means that the junction is effectively blind. At a Stop sign you must stop behind the solid white line.

TIP
The Stop sign is the only road sign that is octagonal in shape.

CLOSED JUNCTIONS

Most junctions are closed junctions, so we'll look at these first.

When you have decided that the junction ahead is a closed junction, you know you will have to slow down or even stop. Brake smoothly and progressively down to a slow walking speed, around 2 or 3mph. Make sure you keep in position as you approach the broken white line that marks the junction, keeping 1m from the kerb if turning left, or close to the centre line if turning right. About two car lengths from the Give Way line change down into first gear and bring the clutch back to biting point. Let the car roll up to the line slowly.

A closed junction

TIP
Remember that you are looking for a safe gap in the traffic, not cars. You can see cars any time – gaps are much rarer.

BLIND JUNCTIONS

If you reach the white line and are still unable to see clearly, the junction is blind. In this situation, inch your way forward. If another vehicle approaches as you are inching forward, stop and wait for a clear gap. Use clutch control to keep the car very slow. Continue to inch forward until you can see far enough to see a safe gap.

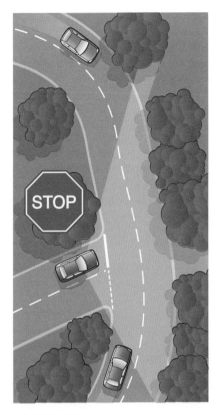

A blind junction

Look

At any junction you must look Right, Left and Right again. These minimum observations ensure that you have seen anything approaching you. If you have to wait for a gap, brake to a stop, set some gas and bring the clutch to the biting point when you see a gap approaching.

Make sure that you check very carefully for less visible road users, such as cyclists and motorcyclists.

If you are turning left, the gap must be big enough to allow you to accelerate to the speed of the traffic you are joining.

If you are turning right, remember that you not only need to have a safe gap to cross traffic approaching from your right, but also a bigger gap to your left so that you have time to accelerate. The gap to your left should be about twice as long as that to your right. If you are turning right, you need to find a safe gap in the oncoming traffic. Try timing the turn on an empty road to see how long it takes you to cross. Counting aloud to yourself 'One Mississippi, two Mississippi' and so on gives a fairly accurate approximation of seconds. If you are turning right and there is oncoming traffic, you will need to add a couple of seconds as a safety margin. Now time the oncoming traffic from a fixed point, such as a lamppost, to the junction. If it takes them longer to reach you than it took you to cross, you will know how far away a vehicle has to be for you to cross safely. If the gap isn't big enough, try counting from another fixed point further away.

Approach the line at the T-junction with your wheels straight, and only start to turn when the front wheels have crossed the line.

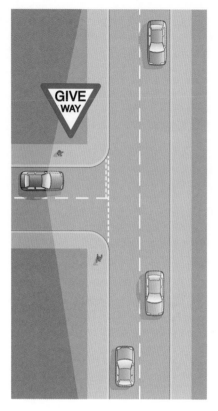

An open junction

OPEN JUNCTIONS

For a junction to be considered open, you must be able to see clearly in both directions that it is safe to continue. Such junctions are actually quite rare, so if you are in any doubt at all, treat it as a closed junction. If you are certain it is safe to proceed, you need to slow down to such a speed that you can turn onto the road accurately and safely. This will very rarely be at more than about 10mph, as you still have to make sure that you are going slowly enough to stop if you have to. At this speed, you will need to select second gear when you are about two car lengths from the line.

Look

Keep looking Right, Left and Right again before crossing the line.

DUAL CARRIAGEWAYS

Turning right to cross a dual carriageway deserves a special mention. As you approach the 'Give Way' line at the junction you must assess whether the central reservation is wide enough for your vehicle to fit fully within the space. If it is wide enough, then you should treat the carriageways as two separate roads. When it is safe, cross to the central reservation and wait there until there is a safe gap on the second half. If the central reservation is not wide enough, you must wait until you can cross both carriageways in one go.

When it is safe, emerge smoothly onto the new road, steering immediately to your normal road position and checking your mirrors to see if anything is closing on you, or about to overtake you. If it is safe, accelerate smoothly away, aiming to match the speed of the other traffic as soon as you reasonably can.

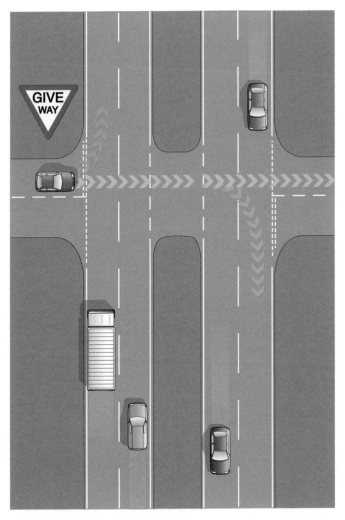

Emerging at a dual carriageway

ROAD MARKINGS AND ROAD SIGNS

It is important that you learn to recognise as many different road marking and signs as you can.

The type of road and traffic signs that you see will highlight what you are expected to do and any likely hazards ahead. There are three main shapes:

- Circles: signs in circles tell you to do (blue) or not do (red) something – they give orders.
- Triangles: signs in triangles tell you of a hazard ahead – they give warnings.
- Rectangles: signs in rectangles tell you about where you are or where you are going – they give information.

Reading these signs correctly will help you understand what is ahead and what kind of junction you are approaching. The same is true of road markings.

For example, you see a white triangle painted on the road surface ahead.

This is a hazard warning sign. It tells you that there is a 'Give Way' junction just ahead. Slow down and be ready to stop.

Practice plan

First steps
On quiet roads, practise emerging at closed junctions. Start by turning left and, when you are reasonably confident, move on to turning right. It is likely that you will be practising both emerging and turning at the same time, so try to find a block where there are both places to turn and places to emerge, thus avoiding the need to turn around.

Gaining confidence
As you gain confidence with the procedure, practise on busier roads, including open and blind junctions.

Ready for the test
You should now practise emerging at all types of junctions, including crossing dual carriageways. Aim to keep moving at Give Way lines if at all possible. Make sure that you select the correct speed and gear, and that your observations are thorough. Never take any risks – if you are not 100% certain that it is safe, stop and wait until you are certain.

Checklist

First steps	Gaining confidence	Ready for the test	
☐	☐		Spotting the signs
☐	☐		Use of MSM/PSL
☐	☐		Signalling correctly/ properly timed
☐	☐		Correct position
☐	☐		Assessing open/closed
☐	☐		Correct speed and gear
☐	☐		Observations
☐	☐		Give Way/Stop
☐	☐		Dual carriageways

1

A junction is a point where t __ __
o__ m__ __ __ r__ __ __ __ __ meet.

Complete the sentence

2

Here are five types of junction.
Name them

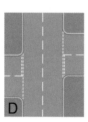

3

Match these road signs to the
junctions shown opposite.

Put letters A, B, C, D and E in the boxes

1 ☐

2 ☐

3 ☐

4 ☐

5 ☐

4

What do these signs mean?

1 Stop and give way

2 Slow down, look, and proceed if safe

3 Give way to traffic on the major road

Put a number in each box

A ☐

B ☐

5

At every junction you should follow a safe routine.

Put the following into the correct order by numbering the boxes 1 to 5

Signal ☐ Speed ☐ Position ☐
Mirrors ☐ Look ☐

6

These are the golden rules for emerging from junctions.

Complete the sentences

1 Always use your m__ __ __ __ __ __ to check the speed and p__ __ __ __ __ __ __ of vehicles behind.

2 Always cancel your s__ __ __ __ __ .

3 Speed up to a s__ __ __ speed after joining the new road.

4 Keep a s__ __ __ d__ __ __ __ __ __ __ between you and the vehicle ahead.

5 Do not attempt to o__ __ __ __ __ __ __ until you can assess the new road.

7

Some junctions have a stop sign, others have a give way sign.

Complete the sentence
A stop sign is usually placed at a junction where v__ __ __ __ __ is l__ __ __ __ __ __.

8

What do these lines across the road mean?

A

1 Stop and give way

2 Give priority to traffic coming from the immediate right.

3 Give way to traffic coming from the right.

Answer ☐

B

1 Give way to traffic on the major road.

2 Stop at the line and give way to traffic on the major road.

Answer ☐

Section 6

EMERGENCY STOP

You must be able to stop the car as quickly as possible under full control, as if in an emergency. You should imagine a child has run out in front of you, and respond accordingly.

How to do it

There are five basic elements to the emergency stop, although in reality these will happen so quickly it will feel like one process: mirrors, steering, brake/clutch, secure vehicle, and observations before moving away.

Do brake firmly and progressively as soon as possible. The brakes will work much more effectively if you squeeze the pedal than if you stamp on it. Remember that as you brake hard your weight will be thrown forward, putting still more pressure on the pedal. Keep your heel on the floor and swivel your foot from the gas to the brake, rather than lifting your whole leg.

Do keep a firm hold of the steering wheel until you stop. When you are braking hard the slightest change of road surface, such as a manhole cover or large stone, may cause the car to pull sharply to one side.

Do press the clutch pedal down just before you stop. As long as the clutch is up, engine braking will help slow the car down. If you de-clutch too soon, you will lose this extra braking and the car will take longer to stop. Stopping in time is much more important than keeping the engine going.

> **LEGAL REQUIREMENTS**
> You'll find the typical stopping distances in *The Highway Code*, rule 126. You must know these for your Theory Test, but you should also have practical experience of how far you will actually travel when stopping in an emergency. You also need to be familiar with the section on braking, rules 117–121.

Do apply the handbrake and select neutral as soon as the car is stationary, Any following vehicle may not stop so quickly, and could therefore run into you. In this case, the handbrake will prevent you from being pushed too far forward, into the child you just managed to avoid. Selecting neutral will prevent the same scenario if your foot slips off the clutch pedal.

Do make sure it is safe to drive on. Look all around the car and double-check your right and left blind spots. Remember, you will have a 1m gap to your left – enough for a cyclist to get through; also, you can expect people to run towards you to check that the child is all right.

Don't check your mirrors as you will not have time to. A good driver checks their mirrors regularly and so will already know what is behind them. Besides, even if there is a vehicle too close behind, it is better to have them run into you than for you to run into the child.

Don't attempt to steer away from the child. You need the total available grip of the tyres on the road to stop the car. If you attempt to steer you will use up some of that grip in turning, meaning either that you run out of grip and therefore skid, or that you take longer to stop because you cannot brake as hard.

In summary then:
• Brake quickly, firmly and progressively. Clutch down at the last moment.
• Keep a firm grip on the wheel and steer straight.
• Handbrake and neutral as soon as you stop.
• All round observations, double-check both blind spots before driving away.
• No mirror check.

SKID CONTROL
A skid is caused by the tyres losing their grip on the road and sliding across the surface. If this happens when braking, the vehicle will take longer to stop and the driver may lose control, so it is important to correct the skid immediately. When skidding in a straight line, simply apply less pressure on the pedal.

If the car starts to slide sideways, you need to ease off the pressure on the footbrake and steer quickly and smoothly in the direction of the skid. So, if the rear of the car is sliding to the right, steer to the right.

TIP
Anti-lock braking systems (ABS) allow you to steer while braking hard, avoiding a skid in most cases. Note that ABS cannot totally prevent a skid.

What to do if you skid: if the rear of the car skids to the right, turn the steering wheel into the skid to bring the vehicle back under control

AWARENESS AND PLANNING

Knowing how to stop the car in an emergency is a vital skill. More important still is driving so that you never have to make an emergency stop. A good driver drives at such a speed that they can always stop comfortably. This skill is a product of awareness, planning and anticipation. We shall discuss these key elements of driving skills in later sections, but for now, it is important that you are aware of the need to make sure you are never driving too fast for the road and traffic conditions.

Think about the area in which you are driving. What sort of hazards are you likely to meet – for example, pedestrians in built-up areas, children or pets running out in residential areas, slow-moving vehicles emerging from hidden junctions in rural areas? Is the time of day – such as school or pub closing times – likely to be a factor?

By planning for such possibilities, you should be able to avoid having to make an emergency stop.

Remember, too, to consider the factors that may affect your braking:

- You are the major factor in the equation. If your eyesight isn't all it could be, you may not see the hazard as early as you should. If you are tired or 'under the weather', your reaction time may be slower.
- Drugs and alcohol have an enormous impact on reaction times. In some people, just one unit of alcohol can more than double their reaction time. Remember, the message is 'don't drink and drive', not 'don't drink a lot and drive'. You may still pass a breathalyser test, but your reaction time may be dangerously increased.
- Prescription medicines or over-the-counter remedies may also have a serious effect on your state of alertness or reactions. If you are taking any medicines, make sure you check with your doctor or pharmacist before driving.
- Road and weather conditions are a further factor to consider. In poor visibility or at night you may not see hazards as soon as you could in clear daylight, so slow down. Rain, mist, snow and ice will all affect your grip on the road, so you'll need to increase the gap in front of you and slow down if necessary.

- The condition of your vehicle is also a crucial factor. Make certain that your brake pads, brake discs, brake fluid and hoses, tyres and suspension are all in perfect order. These should be checked when your car is serviced properly, but in between services you will need to check these yourself.

TIP
If you realise that your car is starting to skid, ease off the brake and accelerator, then steer smoothly in the same direction as the skid.

WHEN TO DO IT

Finally, you need to consider when you may need to make an emergency stop. You should only use this stopping technique when human life is in danger – and that includes your own life.

However, should you use it to stop for a sparrow, cat, dog, sheep, deer or horse?

To answer this you must use some common sense and consider the size of the animal. Will it put your own life at risk? Before stopping for smaller animals, make sure you are not compromising the safety of humans, such as the occupants of the vehicle following you. Check your mirrors first and only if it is safe, brake hard.

Practice plan

First steps
Make sure you practise on a quiet road and be certain that it is safe before every stop.

Begin by stopping slowly from about 15mph. Don't brake too hard at first, so you have time to reinforce the correct procedure and sequence of actions. Remember to brake as quickly as possible, but leave the clutch up as long as you can.

Gaining confidence
When you are happy with the routine, gradually increase your speed and the firmness of your braking. Aim to get to 30mph before stopping. You should test how hard you can brake before the ABS cuts in or the wheels lock. Remember to ease off the pressure on the footbrake if you start to skid.

Ready for the test
Practise on different road surfaces and in different weather conditions, remembering to make sure it is safe first. Try to ensure you get plenty of practice in the rain or when there is a frost.

Checklist

First steps	Gaining confidence	Ready for the test	
☐	☐	☐	Quick reaction
☐	☐	☐	Firm, progressive braking
☐	☐	☐	No mirrors
☐	☐	☐	No steering
☐	☐	☐	Handbrake, neutral
☐	☐	☐	Observations and blind spots
☐	☐	☐	Poor road surfaces
☐	☐	☐	Poor weather conditions
☐	☐	☐	Skid control
☐	☐	☐	Understanding of factors
☐	☐	☐	Anticipation, awareness and planning

1

Are the following statements true or false when stopping in an emergency?

Tick the appropriate boxes   **True**   **False**

1 Stopping in an emergency increases the risk of skidding. ☐ ☐

2 I should push the brake pedal down harder as I slow down. ☐ ☐

3 It is important to. react quickly ☐ ☐

4 I should always remember to look in my mirrors as I slow down. ☐ ☐

5 I should signal left to tell other road users what I am doing. ☐ ☐

6 I should keep both hands on the wheel. ☐ ☐

7 I should always check my mirrors and look round before moving off. ☐ ☐

2

Is the following statement true or false?

An emergency stop will be carried out on every driving test

Tick the correct box   **YES** ☐   **NO** ☐

3

Anti-lock braking systems (ABS)* are fitted to most modern cars.

Fill in the missing words
When braking in an emergency, ABS brakes allow you to s__ __ __ __ and b__ __ __ __ at the same time.

Are these statements about ABS braking true or false?

Tick the appropriate boxes   **True**   **False**

1 Cars fitted with ABS braking cannot skid. ☐ ☐

2 I do not need to leave as much room between me and the car in front if I have ABS brakes because I know I can stop in a shorter distance. ☐ ☐

*ABS is a registered trade mark of Bosch (Germany). ABS stands for Anti-Blockiersystem. The English translation is Anti-lock Braking System

4

In wet weather conditions your tyres can lose their grip. You should allow at least d__ __ __ __ __ the distance between you and the car in front that you allow on a dry road.

Fill in the missing word

5

Will less tread on your tyres...

Tick the correct box

1 Increase your braking distance? ☐

2 Decrease your braking distance? ☐

6

When the tyres lose contact with the road, the steering will feel v__ __ __ l__ __ __ __.

Complete the sentence

7

Is the following statement about anti-lock brakes true or false?

Anti-lock brakes will stop me skidding when driving on snow or ice.

Tick the correct box **True** ☐ **False** ☐

8

When driving in snow or ice you should gently test your b__ __ __ __ __ from time to time.

Fill in the missing word

9

Three important factors cause a skid.

Name them.

1 _____

_____

2 _____

_____

3 _____

_____

10

Some everyday driving actions, especially in poor weather, can increase the risk of skidding.

Fill in the missing words

1 S__ __ __ __ __ __ down.

2 S__ __ __ __ __ __ __ up.

3 T__ __ __ __ __ __ corners.

4 Driving u__ __ __ __ __ and d__ __ __ __ __ __ __.

MSM/PSL – HAZARD ROUTINE

The mirrors – signal – manoeuvre/ position – speed – look routine (usually shortened to MSM/PSL) is fundamental to learning to drive. You must use it before you might have to make any change of speed or direction. It is often called the 'hazard routine', because you must use it whenever you see a hazard.

How to do it

The MSM routine helps you execute manoeuvres safely and under full control.

Two definitions may help make this clearer: A manoeuvre is any change of speed or direction. A hazard is anything that may cause you to manoeuvre – that is, to change your speed or direction.

The important word here is 'may'. You might be able to negotiate some hazards without actually having to change speed or direction at all, but the potential danger is there, so you must always be prepared in case the situation changes suddenly.

'Mirrors–signal–manoeuvre' reminds you to check your mirrors and give a signal before you make any change of speed or direction. By definition, you will use the routine every time you spot a hazard.

MIRRORS

As soon as you spot the hazard, you must check your mirrors. The main mirror shows the road behind you. If there is a vehicle travelling too close to you, you may have to give an earlier signal so that it has time to drop back before you slow down.

The right door mirror shows if anything is attempting to overtake you. If you intend to move to the right, you must check that it is safe before you signal.

LEGAL REQUIREMENTS
Information and laws relating to the MSM/PSL hazard routine appear throughout *The Highway Code*.

TIP
Imagine that a motorcyclist is about to overtake you. If you give a signal as they pull out, it may cause them to swerve or brake hard, and they could possibly lose control. By checking your right mirror in good time, you can allow them to complete their overtaking manoeuvre before you signal your intention to slow down, turn or whatever.

In the same way, you must check the left door mirror before signalling left. This is especially important when you are in slower traffic, as cyclists have the opportunity to pass on your left. Again, you must check your mirrors in good time, so that you can allow time to give an earlier signal or delay your signal as appropriate.

SIGNAL

At this stage of the routine you must decide if a signal is necessary – sometimes it may not be required. Signals are made to tell other road users of your intentions – if you are alone on an empty road, with no other road users in sight, a signal may not be necessary.

Having made sure it is safe, you need to signal your intentions to other road users. If you intend to change direction then you may use your direction indicators. However, there are many other signals besides your indicators that you can use.

Can you spot all the potential hazards for the red car in this scene?

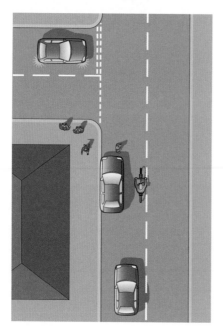

For example, your brake lights indicate to following vehicles that you are slowing down or stopping. By gently touching the brake pedal, you can light the brake lights without slowing down too much. However, this should give a driver who is following too closely enough time to brake and drop back before you brake more firmly and slow down.

Your position in the road can also be seen as a signal. This is particularly useful when you're overtaking a parked car. If you pull out smoothly, well before you need to pass the obstruction, you allow any following vehicle to see the obstruction. They will then expect you to go around it, so you have effectively signalled your intentions. As well as informing following vehicles of your intentions, pulling out in good time allows oncoming vehicles to see you sooner and allows you to get a clearer view past the obstruction.

TIP
Using the right indicator when passing parked vehicles can be misleading – where there are parked cars there are often more junctions too, and an indicator could be seen as meaning that you intend to turn right.

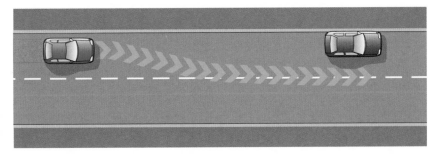

Pull out in plenty of time to pass a parked vehicle

You must take care that you do not give two conflicting signals – for example, by indicating left but positioning yourself to the right of your lane. This may confuse other road users, and could cause them to misinterpret your intentions.

Try to put yourself in the shoes of others – how would you read signal described above if you were in the car behind?

You must always signal in good time, so that other road users have time to make their own changes of speed or direction smoothly. If you need to delay indicating because of a side road or parked car, consider other signals you could use. Could you use your position to show you are overtaking and then indicate when you are positioned to the right? Could you use your brake lights to show that you are slowing before you reach the side road, and indicate left as you pass it to show that you are taking the next road off?

Arm signals can also be useful to help make your intentions clear. For example, if you lived in a corner house where your driveway was just before a side road, others could misinterpret your right indicator signal to mean you are taking the side road. Using an arm signal in this instance to reinforce the signals given by your indicators and brake lights would make it clear to other road users that you are doing something out of the ordinary, and they would be more likely to keep back.

TIP
You need to be familiar with all the signals shown in *The Highway Code*, not only so that you can use them properly, but also so that you understand the intentions of other road users when they use them.

Use arm signals to make your intentions clear

I intend to slow down or stop

I intend to move in to the left or turn left

I intend to move out to the right or turn right

I want to turn left; use either hand

MANOEUVRE

The third part of MSM, the manoeuvre itself, is divided into three more phases: PSL, or position–speed–look.

POSITION

You need to position your vehicle properly in the road. Whenever you intend to turn left, you should maintain your normal road position, about 1m from the kerb or left-hand side of the

road. You must not swing out to make a wider turn as you take the corner – having signalled left, you must not then move right, as other vehicles may be about to overtake you.

If you intend to turn right, you should take up a position as close to the centre line as is safe. On a wider road, this allows following traffic to pass on your left and confirms your indicated signal.

Remember you have blind spots (shown in red) to both left and right

SPEED

Now you need to get to the correct speed. Always judge your speed according to what you can or can't see. A rough guide is that you should never be going faster than 1mph for 1m you can see along your intended route. For example, if you approach a tight left turn where you can only see 9m around the corner, then you should proceed at no more than 9mph. This will allow you time to stop comfortably if there is a problem just beyond your line of sight.

You can practice judging distances near your home (a good stride is about 1m). Pace out the distances between familiar landmarks so that you have references for 10m, 20m, 30m and 50m.

Always brake to the speed that you want before changing into the appropriate gear for that speed. Avoid changing gear while you are still braking, and remember to slow down soon enough that you have time to change gear before starting to steer.

LOOK

Just before starting to steer, about two car lengths away, look in the door mirror in the direction you intend to steer. There could be a cyclist about to pass on your left or someone about to overtake on your right. Also look where you intend to go. If turning left or right, you need to be certain that there are no pedestrians about to cross as you turn. If necessary, stop before you start to turn – it would be very dangerous to stop half-way through the turn, with your car in a vulnerable position.

A large part of the following sections is concerned with the application of the MSM/PSL routine for specific circumstances. It is vital that you get used to using the routine as soon as possible.

TIP

Observation means looking all around and seeing anything that matters. Don't stare at just one thing – keep your eyes moving.

Practice plan

First steps

Practise judging distances (in metres) in your local area, e.g. from your front door to the house opposite; from your drive to the end of the road; or the distance between the lampposts.

Practise the MSM hazard routine by talking aloud through the routine on quiet roads. Concentrate on the major hazards only – those that will definitely make you change speed or direction. For example, to overtake a parked vehicle you may say: 'Parked car on my side. Checking main and right mirrors – all clear. Signal not needed. Position out to pass one metre away. Speed a little slower for the narrower gap. Looking in my left mirror to check I'm past and pulling back in.'

Don't worry that you're talking in a verbal shorthand, you will need to keep it short in order to have time to say it all.

Gaining confidence

As you become more proficient, try to include the minor hazards as well – those that might make you change speed or direction. You may find that you never manage to complete the whole sequence. If there are so many hazards that you only ever manage to say 'Mirrors, signal... mirrors, signal' then you may need to slow down. Remember, you speak about five times more slowly than you can think, so reciting the routine aloud forces you to do things more slowly.

Practise in busier areas where there are more major hazards. As well as reciting the routine, try to say what could happen with minor hazards, for example: 'Dog on left, off the lead – could run across road so Mirrors – car close behind so Signal with brake lights. Position – move further from kerb and Speed – slowing in case. Looking that I'm safely past.'

Ready for the test

By now you should be at ease with reciting the routine aloud. Try to run fully through the sequence for every hazard. You should be able to prioritise the various hazards and be prepared to respond to any that develop. Practise spotting the hazards as soon as you can. Scan as far ahead as possible so that you have time to run the full sequence.

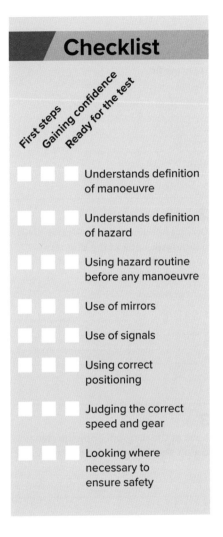

Checklist

First steps	Gaining confidence	Ready for the test	
☐	☐	☐	Understands definition of manoeuvre
☐	☐	☐	Understands definition of hazard
☐	☐	☐	Using hazard routine before any manoeuvre
☐	☐	☐	Use of mirrors
☐	☐	☐	Use of signals
☐	☐	☐	Using correct positioning
☐	☐	☐	Judging the correct speed and gear
☐	☐	☐	Looking where necessary to ensure safety

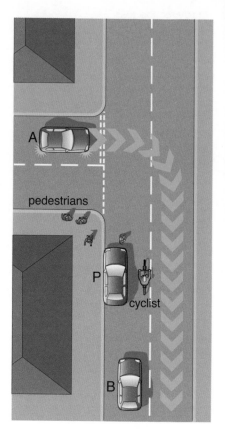

1

Good observation is vital in today's busy traffic.

Complete the sentence

When using my mirrors I should try to make a mental note of the s__ __ __ __, b__ __ __ __ __ __ __ __ and i__ __ __ __ __ __ __ __ __ of the driver behind.

2

Driving in built-up areas is potentially dangerous. Look at the diagram opposite. What action should the driver of car A take?

List four options

1 _____

2 _____

3 _____

4 _____

3

Look at the diagram opposite. What action should the driver of car B take?

List four options

1 _____

2 _____

3 _____

4 _____

4

Some hazards are potential, others are actual and there all the time, such as a bend in the road. Name five more actual hazards.

1 _____
_____

2 _____
_____

3 _____
_____

4 _____
_____

5 _____
_____

_____

5

Name five potential hazards, such as a dog off its lead

1 _____
_____

2 _____
_____

3 _____
_____

4 _____
_____

5 _____
_____

6

Modern driving requires full concentration to be able to spot both actual and potential hazards. Are the following statements true or false?

Tick the correct boxes

	True	False
1 Carrying a mobile phone can reduce the stress of a long journey.	☐	☐
2 It is illegal to use a hand-held mobile phone while driving.	☐	☐
3 Conversation on a hands-free phone can still distract my attention.	☐	☐
4 I should pull up in a safe place to make or receive calls.	☐	☐
5 I should programme my satnav before setting off on my journey.	☐	☐
6 It's safe to adjust my satnav whilst driving.	☐	☐

DEALING WITH TRAFFIC

You need to be able to deal with
situations that involve other road users
– including meeting traffic, crossing a
line of traffic, overtaking other vehicles
and queuing. In any situation you should
not, either by your action or inaction,
cause any other road user to change
speed or direction.

How to do it

MEETING TRAFFIC

A 'meeting' situation is one where an obstruction has narrowed the road so much that only one vehicle can pass at a time. The rules of priority here are very simple: if the obstruction is on your side of the road, you must give priority to oncoming traffic – that is, let drivers on the other side of the road through first. The same thing applies in reverse: if your side of the road is clear, you have priority over oncoming traffic. However, you must never assume that the oncoming vehicle is going to let you through first.

When you are assessing the gap, think about the speed, position and size of the oncoming vehicle. You may choose to allow a large lorry or bus through, even when you have priority, as it would be much more difficult for them to stop than for you. Sometimes the rules of priority conflict with each other. For example, if a large, fully laden lorry was coming up a hill towards you and the obstruction was on their side of the road, you might allow them priority. When being considerate like this, don't forget about the traffic behind you. The lorry driver may think you are a considerate driver – but the six vehicles stuck behind you may not agree.

The **MSM/PSL** routine is your guide to how to handle meeting an obstruction **on your side** of the road.

LEGAL REQUIREMENTS

The Highway Code has rules and advice for a variety of situations such as:
- slow-moving traffic: rule 151
- single track roads: rules 155–156
- overtaking: rules 162–169
- crossing: rules 170, 173, 174, 179–181
- road works: rules 288–290.

Mirrors

As soon as you see the obstruction ahead, check your main mirror to look out for following traffic, and your right mirror if you will need to pull out to pass.

You must now decide who has priority. If oncoming traffic has priority, you must give way and allow the oncoming vehicles to come through first.

Signal

You will signal to other road users by your position on the road, as using your indicators in this case could cause confusion – the oncoming vehicle may think you intend to force your way through.

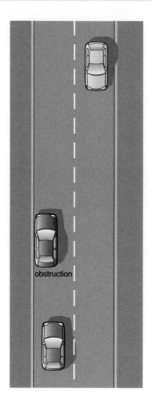 

Priority in a meeting situation: in the picture on the left, the yellow car has priority over the red car; in the right-hand picture, the red car has priority over the lorry, as the obstruction is on the opposite side of the road

Position

Pull out slightly to your right to allow yourself a clear view past the obstruction, but only so far that any oncoming vehicle can pass you safely. Not only do you get a better view ahead, but also following traffic will now be able to see the obstruction and will know what you are doing.

Speed

Slow down enough so that, if possible, the oncoming vehicle has time to pass through the gap before you are forced to stop. As soon as there is a safe gap, steer out to pass the obstruction.

Of course, there may be more than one oncoming vehicle and you may have to stop. In this case take up the 'holdback position', about two car lengths behind the obstruction and as far to the right as is safe. This position makes it easier to see and be seen, as well as leaving room for you to pull out briskly when there is a safe gap. If you get too close to the obstruction, you will need to use much more steering and therefore will have to emerge more slowly, requiring a bigger gap.

Look

Keep looking past the obstruction for a safe gap, and checking your mirrors to make sure a following vehicle isn't going to overtake you as you pull out. Make sure you leave enough room to pass the obstruction safely: if it is a vehicle a door may open, or if it is a builder's skip someone might step out from behind it. Try to anticipate the possible hazards and plan for them. If you must get closer than 1m, make sure that you are travelling slowly enough to be able to stop.

Use your left mirror to check when you are past the obstruction and pull back into your normal road position as soon as possible.

If the obstruction is on the **opposite** side of the road and you have priority, you will still use the MSM/PSL routine. However, you must be prepared to stop in case an oncoming vehicle is going to force its way through.

Mirrors

Check your main mirror and left mirror, in case you need to slow down or pull over to your left.

Signal

You may need to use your brake lights to show following traffic that you are slowing down. Again, your speed and position will act as a signal to oncoming traffic.

Position

Maintain your normal road position for as long as you can – pulling over to the left could be misinterpreted by oncoming traffic as 'I'm making room for you'.

Speed

Slow down a little, as you have to pass through a narrow gap. However, try not to slow down so much that oncoming drivers think you are stopping to allow them through.

Look

Constantly reassess the speed and position of oncoming vehicles. If it looks as if they are going to force their way through, make sure you are in a position to stop safely.

CROSSING TRAFFIC

Nearly every time you turn right from a major road, you are crossing the path of other traffic. It is essential that you can do this safely, and without causing any other road user to take any type of action.

In Section 4 you read about turning at junctions and how you might judge a safe gap.

If it would be safe to walk across the road in front of an oncoming vehicle, it is almost certainly safe to drive across. You should have had plenty of practice as a pedestrian, but if you are still hesitant about timing, try the following method.

See how long it takes you to drive across a quiet road from a standing start. Counting 'One Mississippi, two Mississippi' and so on as you do this gives a fairly accurate approximation of the number of seconds it takes you. Now add a couple of seconds as a safety margin. The resulting total is how long a gap you would need to cross safely.

Now time the oncoming traffic from a fixed point, such as a lamppost, to the junction. If it takes them longer to reach you than it took you to cross, that is a safe gap. If the gap isn't big enough, try counting from another fixed point further away. Try to make a mental note of the distance – compare it to some familiar landmark such as the distance from your front door to the end of the street. As you practise, you will get better at judging these distances, but always be aware of speeding traffic or faster speed limits.

> **TIP**
> Remember to look out for signals given by other road users. While you cannot always trust a signal given by another road user – wait until you see it confirmed by a change in speed or direction – it may help you spot a gap earlier.

When crossing dual carriageways, you must first decide whether the central reservation is wide enough for you to stop in if necessary. If you can fit your vehicle in the space without overhanging the central reservation, then you should treat the dual carriageway as two separate roads. Cross to the central reservation when it is safe, and wait there until it is safe to continue to the other side (see diagram, page 59). Remember, if there is more than one lane, you should always join the left-hand lane of traffic at first, allowing yourself time to build up your speed.

If the central reservation is not wide enough, you must wait until it is safe to cross both carriageways in one go. In this case be careful to allow enough time to join the stream of traffic on your left.

OVERTAKING

Whenever you pass another road user, whether they are stationary or moving, you are overtaking. As for most situations, you will use the MSM/PSL routine to help you, but in this particular situation it is slightly modified: before the main MSM/PSL you need to do an additional MPSL in order to get a good view of the road ahead. The routine now becomes **MPSL/MSM/PSL**. This routine is exactly the same whether you are overtaking stationary or moving vehicles, so we will assume we are overtaking a moving vehicle – in this case a lorry.

First, you must decide whether the overtaking manoeuvre is necessary, legal and safe.

Is it necessary? Do you intend to turn off soon? Is the vehicle you intend to overtake signalling to turn off? Are you going to be going faster than them after overtaking? Think about the possibilities – for example, if you are behind a bus, is it likely to stop soon for passengers to get on or off? Use local knowledge – for example, if you are behind a large truck, you may know it is likely to turn off into a quarry in half a mile. Look at road signs – you may see a 'Dual carriageway ahead in 1 mile' sign.

Is it legal? Would you need to cross a solid white line on your side of the centre line?

Would you have to exceed the speed limit in order to pass safely?

Is it safe? Can you see far enough ahead to see a safe gap? Are there any junctions ahead?

As long as you can satisfy these three requirements and are certain that there is no risk involved, then you may start the overtaking procedure.

MPSL
As soon as you can see that you are closing up on the lorry, check your mirrors and position yourself so that you have a good view of the road ahead. You may also need to change down to a lower gear to get more acceleration at the speed you are doing.

In some situations, it may help your planning to move to the left to look past the vehicle. This will allow you to spot any parked obstructions ahead, and you will be able to anticipate the lorry moving out. It is also important that you keep well back, particularly for large vehicles, as this will give you a better view of the road ahead.

Mirrors
Check your main mirror and right mirror. As always, you are checking to see if there is anything there that may prevent you from signalling or cause you to delay your manoeuvre, such as a motorbike overtaking you. Consider a sideways glance, especially on multi-lane roads.

Signal
If it is safe, indicate right to show that you intend to pull out.

Position

When you are sure it is safe to do so, pull out. Time this so that you are still a safe distance behind the lorry in case you need to pull back in. You will now have a clear view ahead.

TIP
Make sure you leave plenty of room when overtaking cyclists, horses or motorbikes, as they are much more likely to move sideways, especially in windy conditions.

Speed

If it is still safe, accelerate so that you pass the lorry briskly, but without breaking the speed limit.

Look

Use your left mirror and main mirror to check that you are safely past the lorry before pulling back into your normal road position. You will be safely past the lorry when you can see the whole of the front of it in your main mirror. You must avoid cutting in after overtaking – try to give the lorry a two-second gap if possible.

After overtaking, make sure you don't accidentally slow down again, which would cause the lorry behind to have to brake.

If you changed down a gear to go past, don't forget to use the appropriate gear at the new speed.

QUEUING TRAFFIC

When driving in slow-moving queues of traffic you have an opportunity to practise clutch control and demonstrate awareness of the spaces around you. Avoid stop-start driving by using clutch control to keep your car moving slowly (see Section 3).

Look ahead as far as possible and anticipate what the traffic in front of you is likely to do. Instead of just watching the rear of the vehicle immediately in front of you, try to watch the roof or brake lights of the vehicle about five or six cars in front. By doing this you will get advance warning of the queue stopping.

Make sure you leave a reasonable gap between you and the car in front. This gap shouldn't be excessive – that will only encourage others to jump in – but leave yourself room to get a better view ahead.

You must never get so close that you are unable to see clear road ahead of you. Use the 'Tyres and Tarmac' rule: you should stop at a point when you can still see the tyres of the vehicle in front touching the road, plus about 1m of tarmac.

If an emergency vehicle came from behind, you would have enough room to pull over to the left to let it pass. If the vehicle in front broke down, you would be able to pull out to pass it with ease.

Leave the entrances to side roads clear, so that oncoming traffic can turn off easily, avoiding a queue forming in the other direction as well. It is especially important that you never stop on a pedestrian crossing – always wait until you have enough room in front to clear the crossing. The same rule applies to junctions and roundabouts: wait behind the line until you can clear the junction.

Remember to use your handbrake when you stop, especially at night, as keeping your foot on the footbrake will dazzle the driver of the vehicle behind.

TIP

If the queue is stationary for a long time – five minutes or more – consider turning off your engine. A stationary car emits a lot of noxious fumes, even at idling speed – and with the engine off, you'll save some fuel, too.

Practice plan

First steps
Meeting – Practise on quiet roads at first, concentrating on judging the width of road remaining: is there enough room for two cars to pass? Practise slowing down and getting going again on an empty road, before repeating the exercise with parked cars but no oncoming traffic. Use MSM/PSL out loud.

Crossing – You will already have practised turning to the right – make sure you are confident in your judgement and execution of the basic procedure.

Overtaking – At first it is likely that you will only overtake slow-moving vehicles such as road-sweepers, cyclists and tractors. Try to ensure you get plenty of practice overtaking these slower moving vehicles.

Queuing – It may seem silly to choose to drive in traffic jams, but that is what you need to do. Try to find small jams, or roads where there are plenty of escape routes. Temporary road works in towns are usually a good option. Practise clutch control and positioning, with special attention to keeping moving if at all possible.

Gaining confidence

Meeting – Practise in residential areas where there are plenty of parked cars and a reasonable amount of traffic. Concentrate on keeping a sufficient distance away from the obstructions, and judging your speed of approach so that you can keep moving whenever possible.

Crossing – Make sure your practice includes crossing dual carriageways and busy areas where there is a lot of pedestrian activity.

Overtaking – Practise overtaking on dual carriageways, where there is no danger from oncoming vehicles. Make sure you take any opportunity to overtake without first slowing down.

Queuing – Try to include at least one major queue in each practice session. The approaches to major road junctions during the rush hour will provide realistic practice.

Ready for the test

Meeting – Practise on busy urban roads. You should aim to keep moving, if appropriate, by adjusting your speed and position as early as you can.

Crossing – You should aim to take smaller, but safe, gaps in moving traffic and be ready to act on signals given by other road users. Always be prepared to take the opportunity to go if someone shows they are letting you go first, but make sure it is safe before taking any action.

Overtaking – Lots of practice on major rural roads should give you the opportunity to overtake on single carriageways at speed. This, however, is increasingly rare as our roads are so busy. Try to maximise your chances by using wide roads with long straights if possible – usually those with only one or two digits in their names e.g. A19, A56.

Queuing – Driving through a busy town centre during rush hour will provide all the practice you need.

Checklist

	First steps	Gaining confidence	Ready for the test

Meeting

			Recognise meeting situations early
			Understand rules of priority
			Judging a safe gap
			Use of MSM/PSL
			Correct use of position
			Correct use of speed
			Adequate clearance to obstructions

Crossing

			Judging a safe gap
			Keeping moving where possible
			Acting on the signals of other road users
			Crossing dual carriageways

	First steps	Gaining confidence	Ready for the test

Overtaking

			Necessary?
			Legal?
			Safe?
			Use of MPSL/MSM/PSL
			Use of correct gear
			Maintaining speed

Queuing

			Clutch control
			Following distance
			Keeping moving where possible
			'Tyres and Tarmac' rule
			Clearance for junctions, pedestrian crossings
			Engine off for long waits
			Use of handbrake

1

Before overtaking, consider whether it is really n_ _ _ _ _ _ _ _.

Fill in the missing word

2

Always use the safety routine when overtaking.

Put these actions into their correct sequence for the diagram by putting numbers 1 to 7 in the boxes

☐ Signal ☐ Mirrors ☐ Look
☐ Position ☐ Mirrors ☐ Speed
☐ Manoeuvre

3

The diagram shows a stationary vehicle on the left-hand side of the road.

Which should have priority, vehicle 1 or vehicle 2?

Answer ☐

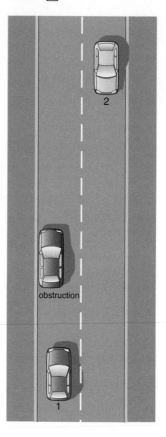

4

This diagram shows a steep downward hill with an obstruction on the right-hand side of the road.

Which vehicle should be given priority, vehicle 1 or vehicle 2?

Answer ☐

5

Where you see double solid white lines painted along the centre of the road, what does this mean?

Tick any boxes you think are appropriate. More than one answer may be correct.

1 I must not park or wait on the carriageway. ☐

2 I can park between 7pm and 7am. ☐

3 I must not overtake. ☐

4 I must not cross the white line except to turn right or in circumstances beyond my control. ☐

PEDESTRIAN AND LEVEL CROSSINGS

You must approach and negotiate pedestrian and level crossings safely and with due regard for other road users. You must know the difference between the various types of road crossings and how to recognise them visually.

How to do it

From your study of Driving Theory, you will know that there are six main types of pedestrian road crossings: zebra, pelican, puffin and toucan crossings, horse and equestrian crossings, and the school crossing controlled by a patrol, or 'lollipop' person. We can separate these into two groups: pedestrian-controlled and light-controlled. Level crossings – where the road crosses a railway track – fall into the 'light-controlled' category.

PEDESTRIAN-CONTROLLED CROSSINGS

The **zebra crossing**, named for the black-and-white stripes on the road. The rules for zebra crossings are very clear:

- If a pedestrian is waiting to cross, you should slow down and stop, if necessary, to allow them to cross.
- If a pedestrian is on the crossing, you MUST give way and allow them to cross. 'On the crossing' means that a pedestrian has only to place one toe on the road and you must stop. This is a legal requirement. For this reason, you must always approach a zebra crossing with the utmost caution and always be prepared to stop.

Zebra crossings are usually found in very busy areas, such as town centres or near schools. You may have little warning that a pedestrian is going to cross, so you must be especially careful.

LEGAL REQUIREMENTS
The section about pedestrian crossings can be found in rules 191–199 of *The Highway Code*. Level crossings follow a similar routine – the rules relating to these run from 291–299.

A zebra crossing is easily distinguished by the orange flashing beacon lightpoles on either side of the crossing and the broad black-and-white stripes on the road surface. In addition, there will be zigzag markings running along either side of the road. All permanent crossings have these zigzags, which indicate that you must neither park within their extent nor overtake the leading moving motor vehicle or a vehicle that is already waiting at the crossing.

The road sign that indicates a zebra crossing ahead

Use the MSM/PSL routine to negotiate the crossing.

Mirrors

As soon as you spot the crossing ahead, check your mirrors, as you will be slowing down. Then, look to see if there are any pedestrians waiting to cross or on the crossing itself. Always check your mirror first, as you may not see a pedestrian stepping out until the last moment – too late to check your mirror.

Signal

Use your brake lights to indicate to any following traffic that you are slowing down.

Position

Maintain your normal road position, but be aware that in busy areas people may step out in the vicinity of the crossing.

Speed

Slow down and be prepared to stop behind the line. Most pedestrians will wait until you are stationary before they cross. If you have to stop, apply the handbrake so that your vehicle is secure.

Look

If pedestrians are using the crossing, don't intimidate them. If the crossing appears to be clear and you are still moving, keep looking to make sure no one steps out at the last moment. Use some common sense when making your observations: pedestrians facing away from the crossing are not likely to use it. Always take great care and make sure you are travelling slowly enough to stop if you need to.

The **school crossing** controlled by a patrol, or lollipop person, is a temporary crossing specifically for the use of schoolchildren and their carers. The patrol has all the powers of a policeman or woman to stop and direct traffic.

Again, the rules are very simple: if the patrol is standing at the kerb with the lollipop raised, traffic must stop and allow them to take up position in the road. When they return to the side of the road and lower the sign, traffic may proceed.

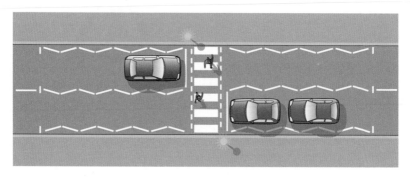

Road markings clearly indicate this is a zebra crossing

The road sign for school crossing patrol ahead (left) and the sign used by a school crossing patrol (right)

Most crossing patrols are well signed. You should see the 'Patrol' warning sign, and possibly flashing amber warning lights when the crossing is being used. These will be positioned about 100m ahead of the crossing – ample distance for you to slow down in preparation. The patrol person will be wearing bright yellow clothing and is easy to spot.

Once again, use the MSM/PSL routine.

Mirrors
As soon as you see the patrol road signs, check your mirrors. Remember that children may cross at other places as well, and are not always good at judging the speed of approaching cars.

TIP
Pre-adolescent children have not yet developed the ability to judge speed accurately, and may think they have plenty of time to cross when, in reality, they don't.

Signal
Use your brake lights to show following vehicles that you are slowing down.

Position
Maintain your normal road position.

Speed
Slow down to a speed at which you can easily stop if necessary.

Look
Look for the patrol person and for other pedestrians crossing near by. If the lollipop is up, make sure you stop well before you reach the crossing patrol. If the lollipop is down, proceed with caution: older children or carers are just as likely to ignore the crossing patrol as to use it. Always be prepared to stop, applying the handbrake as soon as you are stationary if you do need to stop.

LIGHT-CONTROLLED CROSSINGS
The **pelican crossing** (from PEdestrian LIght-CONtrolled) was introduced to make it easier for pedestrians to cross busy roads. As the name suggests, the pedestrians control the traffic lights. Extra care is needed when negotiating these crossings.

To cross the road, a pedestrian must press the button on the light control box which will cause the traffic lights to change. When you see the lights change to amber and then red – the normal sequence, see page 112 – you must stop. You may hear a beeping sound, which is an audible signal for the blind. The pedestrian will see a 'green

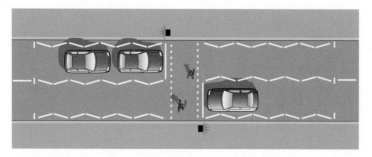

Learn to spot the differences bewteen a pelican and other types of crossings

man' signal allowing them to cross. At some point, the beeping will stop and the pedestrian will see the 'green man' signal flashing. They should not start to cross, but may continue if they were already on the crossing.

Next, you will see your amber light flashing. Like the orange flashing beacon at a zebra crossing, this instructs you to give way to any pedestrians on the crossing, but if the crossing is clear you may proceed.

Your traffic light will then turn green, meaning that you may proceed if it is safe. Remember, you must give way to any pedestrians still crossing, even though your light is green.

When the button is pressed, the interval before the lights change can vary greatly and may be controlled by a traffic sensor. This causes two main problems for you, the driver.

Firstly, an impatient pedestrian may not wait for the lights to change, and will cross as soon as there is a gap in the traffic. Because the button has been pressed, the lights will still change at some point. So, you may approach and see no pedestrians anywhere near the crossing, but the lights could still change. This includes malicious use of the button, where some pedestrians press the button and immediately walk off.

Secondly, if you can see a pedestrian waiting to cross, and maybe even see them pressing the button, you have no idea how long it will be before the lights change in the pedestrians' favour. Because of these problems, you need to approach pelican crossings with particular care.

To identify a pelican crossing, look for the yellow control box mounted on the traffic light post. When the button has been pressed you may be able to see the word 'WAIT' illuminated on the box. As with the zebra crossing, there will be zigzag lines on the road near the crossing. You may also be able to see sensors mounted above the lights, pointing at the traffic.

Use the MSM/PSL routine.

Mirrors

As soon as you identify the crossing or see the lights ahead, check your mirrors. Then look to the sides of the crossing to see if any pedestrians are waiting to cross. If they have pressed the button you may be able to see the 'WAIT' light illuminated on the box.

Signal

Use your brake lights to show following vehicles that you are slowing down.

Position

Maintain your normal road position.

Speed

Slow down to a speed at which you can easily stop if it becomes necessary.

Look

Watch the traffic lights to see if they change to amber. Make sure you also keep watching any pedestrians – if they think you are slowing down because the lights have changed, they may step out, thinking you are stopping. If you do have to stop, wait until the flashing amber light shows, then check if the crossing is clear.

Remember to look out for pedestrians crossing at the last moment. If the crossing is clear, you can proceed before the green light shows.

The **puffin crossing** (from Pedestrian User Friendly INtelligent) avoids the problems associated with pelican crossings by using sensors to monitor the pedestrians. When the button at the roadside is pressed, sensors check if anyone is waiting to cross and will only change the traffic lights if pedestrians are waiting. Sensors also track the pedestrians as they cross the road, so that the lights only change back to green when the crossing is clear. Because of this feature, there is no need for the flashing amber phase.

You can identify a puffin crossing by looking at the lights. You will see sensors mounted above the lights, pointing down at the pedestrian waiting area and crossing, and the button box on the right-hand side of the road will clearly show the red or green man.

As far as you, the driver, are concerned, puffin crossings can be treated in exactly the same way as normal traffic lights:

Mirrors

As soon as you identify the crossing or see the lights, check your mirrors. Then look to the sides of the crossing to see if any pedestrians are waiting to cross. If there are no pedestrians near the crossing the lights are unlikely to change – but the possibility is always there, so you will still slow down as you approach.

Signal

Use your brake lights to show following vehicles that you are slowing down.

Position

Maintain your normal road position.

Speed

Slow down to a speed at which you can stop if necessary.

Look

Keep watching the traffic lights to see if they change to amber. Make sure you also keep watching for pedestrians – they may step out near the crossing. If you do have to stop, wait until the green light shows, then check if the crossing is clear. Remember to look out for pedestrians crossing at the last moment.

The **toucan crossing** (from TOUch CONtrolled, or 'two can' cross) is basically the same as the puffin crossing except that there are two lanes crossing the road – one for pedestrians and another for cyclists.

The light sequence and routine you should follow are identical to the puffin crossing.

One further type of crossing is the **Equestrian crossing**. These light-controlled crossings for horse riders are usually sited near riding schools or stables and work just like a puffin crossing. The button, in this case, is mounted about 2m high so that riders can reach it comfortably without dismounting.

GENERAL RULES FOR PEDESTRIAN CROSSINGS

At any type of crossing you must stop behind the line if required to, and you must never beckon pedestrians to cross – if you wave a pedestrian across, they may not look in the other direction and could be at risk from another vehicle. Neither should you intimidate pedestrians by revving your engine, beeping your horn or moving forwards while they are crossing.

TIP

This is the only type of crossing where cyclists are permitted to ride across the road.

LEVEL CROSSINGS

Level crossings are found where a railway line crosses a road. Most are controlled by light signals and have automatic barriers that come down when a train is coming.

You will see warning signs as you approach the crossing, and should slow down in case there is queuing traffic ahead. At the crossing itself, you will see the lights. If it is safe to pass through the crossing, no lights will show. If a train is approaching, you will first see a solid amber light, which means that you must stop behind the white line. This is shortly followed by flashing red lights and the barriers, if present, will lower automatically. You will also hear an audible signal for pedestrians. You must stop behind the white line and wait for the lights to go off and the barriers to open.

Above: level crossing with (left) and without (right) a gate or barrier

Advance warning of light signals at a level crossing with or without a gate or barrier

If the lights continue to flash after a train has passed, it means that another train is coming. You must continue to wait until the lights cease to flash.

If you should ever break down on a crossing, get everybody out of the vehicle and clear of the crossing, then use the telephone at the crossing to call the signal operator. They will tell you whether it is safe to push the vehicle off the crossing.

Under no circumstances should you ever attempt to rescue the car unless the signal person has authorised it.

If you are in queuing traffic, you must never stop on the level crossing – always wait until there is sufficient space beyond the crossing for you to drive over safely.

TIP

If you have been told it is safe to push the car off the crossing but are on your own, you could put the gear lever into first or reverse and use the ignition key to move the car.

SUMMARY

The key to negotiating any type of crossing is anticipation, awareness and good observation. Try to identify the crossings as early as you can and immediately use your mirrors. Use the MSM/PSL routine as you approach, keep a constant look out for pedestrians and always slow down so that you can stop safely if you have to.

Practice plan

First steps
Practise identifying the various types of crossings from as far away as you can. Say the MSM/PSL routine out loud as you approach.

Gaining confidence
Follow routes that include as many pedestrian crossings as possible. Make sure you follow the MSM/PSL routine and concentrate on acting on what you see: if the crossing is clear as you approach or the lights are still green, try to avoid slowing down too much. Remember, you must always be able to stop if necessary, but you also need to balance this need with making normal progress. Don't take any risks – if you are not sure whether a pedestrian is waiting to cross, it is better to stop than to chance it.

Ready for the test
Try to include level crossings in your routes if possible. Practise developing your anticipation of pedestrian movement and traffic flow at crossings and traffic lights.

Checklist

First steps Gaining confidence Ready for the test

Recognising and negotiating

- Zebra crossings
- Pelican crossings
- Puffin crossings
- Toucan crossings
- School crossing patrols
- Equestrian crossings
- Level crossings
- Anticipation
- Good observations
- Driving at an appropriate speed
- Use of MSM/PSL routine
- Understanding light signals

1

Are these statements about pedestrian crossings true or false?

Tick the correct boxes

	True	False
1 I cannot park or wait on the zig-zag lines on the approach to a zebra crossing.	☐	☐
2 I cannot park or wait on the zig-zag lines on either side of the crossing.	☐	☐
3 I can overtake on the zig-zag lines on the approach to a crossing as long as the other vehicle is travelling slowly.	☐	☐
4 I must give way to a pedestrian once they have stepped on to the crossing.	☐	☐
5 If, on approach to a crossing, I intend to slow down or stop, I may use a slowing-down arm signal.	☐	☐

2

On approaching a pelican crossing, drivers will notice three key features.

Name them

1 _____
_____
_____
_____

2 _____
_____
_____
_____

3 _____
_____
_____
_____

3

The traffic lights at a pelican crossing have the same meaning as ordinary traffic lights, but they do not have a red and amber phase.

1 What do they show instead of the red and amber phase?
Answer _____
_____

2 What does the light mean?
Answer _____
_____

4

What sound is usually heard at a pelican crossing when the green man is shown to pedestrians?

Answer _____

_____

_____

_____

5

Toucan and puffin crossings are similar to pelican crossings but with one main difference. Name it.

Answer _____

_____

_____

_____

6

As well as pedestrians, what other type of road users should you watch for at a toucan crossing?

Answer _____

_____

_____

_____

7

Match each traffic sign below with its correct meaning.

1 Level crossing without gates or barriers ☐

2 Level crossing with lights ☐

3 Level crossing with gates or barriers ☐

4 Level crossing without lights ☐

A   B

KEEP CROSSING CLEAR

GIVE WAY

C

D

8

If you break down on a level crossing, should you...

Tick the appropriate boxes

1 Tell your passengers to wait in the vehicle while you go to get help? ☐

2 Get everybody out and clear of the crossing? ☐

3 Telephone the police? ☐

4 Telephone the signal operator? ☐

5 If there is still time, push your car clear of the crossing? ☐

CROSSROADS

You must be able to recognise, approach and negotiate crossroads safely and with due regard for other road users. You should understand the rules of priority and the differences between marked and unmarked crossroads.

How to do it

A crossroads is usually the junction of a major and a minor road – traffic on the major road will pass through uninterrupted, while that on the minor road will have to stop or give way.

First, let us consider the options if you were on the major road.

ON THE MAJOR ROAD
Going straight ahead

Question: What is the worst thing that could happen as you pass through the crossroads?

Answer: A vehicle could pull straight out in front of you from one of the side roads without seeing you.

It is surprisingly easy to make this mistake if the junction signs are hidden by trees and the lines on the road are faded – especially if you're driving at night and the road is wet and dark. A driver on the minor road would see the road continuing straight ahead of them and may not realise that they are approaching a junction.

LEGAL REQUIREMENTS
The only rule in *The Highway Code* that relates directly to crossroads is rule 181. However, many of the other rules about junctions in general have a bearing on crossroads, including 170–172, 175–178 and 182–183.

TIP
Think of your own experiences as a driver or passenger: have you ever come up to a junction without seeing the signs or markings and only realised at the last moment? This is a very real danger and a scenario which happens all too frequently. In order to minimise the danger, you need to plan for the worst possible case.

About 100m before you reach the crossroads, you should see a triangular sign warning of crossroads ahead (see left). This is your cue to start the MSM/PSL routine.

Mirrors

Check your main mirror to see if anyone is following too closely. If they are, you will need to give a slowing down signal early via your brake lights to encourage them to drop back. Also check your right door mirror, in case you need to pull out further.

Signal

Use your brake lights to show that you are slowing down, but don't press the brake pedal so far down that you slow down too suddenly.

Position

On narrower roads, maintain your normal road position. On a wider road, pull out slightly more from the kerb. This makes it easier for any vehicle emerging from the side road to see you, and gives you a slightly bigger safety margin if one of them pulls out too far over the line. Remember that vehicles emerging from the road on the right may also swing out too far, so pull out from the kerb only as far as it is safe to do so.

Speed

Slow down slightly in case a vehicle does emerge. In a 30mph limit, slowing by 5mph from your original speed should be sufficient. On faster roads reduce your speed by about 10mph. Further explanation of this is given in Section 18.

Look

As you get closer, look into both side roads to see whether any vehicles are approaching the junction. Are they going to emerge, or stop, or give way? Always look into the nearest road first – normally the one on your left – as a vehicle from that direction would be the first to hit you.

TIP
If the worst does happen and a vehicle comes out unexpectedly, make an emergency stop.

As soon as you are safely through the crossroads, gently accelerate back to your original speed.

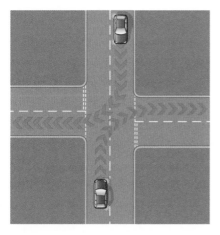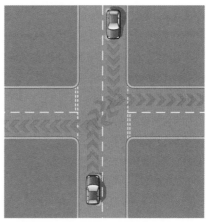

Turning left-side to left-side at a slightly staggered junction (left); turning right-side to right-side at a crossroads (right)

TURNING OFF THE MAJOR ROAD

Turning from the major road into one of the minor roads is essentially the same as turning at a normal junction – except that you need to look into the extra road. Follow the MSM/PSL routine for turning (see Section 4) but add the extra observation to the 'Look' phase. This phase now goes as follows:

- Look into the road you intend to take. You are checking for obstructions that may prevent you from turning. Always give way to pedestrians in the road, stopping on the main carriageway, if necessary, to let them cross.
- Look into the road opposite to be sure that no vehicles are attempting to pull out in front of you.

- You also need to check your door mirrors to be sure that no one is attempting to pass. If you are turning right, someone could be about to overtake, or, if turning left, a cyclist may be about to pass on your left, especially if the traffic is moving slowly.
- A special action is required when both you and a vehicle approaching from directly ahead are turning to your respective right – that is, you are going in opposite directions.

There are two choices here, depending on the exact layout of the road (see above). If the crossroads is staggered and the road you wish to take is nearer to you than the road on your left, then you can pass left-side to left-side (nearside to nearside).

This method will place the other car between you and the road ahead, limiting your view, so you must be very careful. Remember, a motorcyclist could be passing the other car on its left and may be hidden by the other car.

At a straight crossroads, where the roads form a perfect cross, it is safer to pass driver's-side to driver's-side (offside to offside), as this allows you to get a much better view of the road ahead.

The best solution to this problem is to make sure you spot the other vehicle's signal early. You can then slow down enough to give them time to turn before you reach your turning point, thus avoiding the complication completely. Gaining eye contact with the other driver can help you read the situation.

ON THE MINOR ROAD

Turning left or right at a crossroads is again essentially the same as at a T-junction, except for the extra road opposite: you need to include this road in your observations, so the minimum observations become 'Right, Left, Ahead and Right again'.

Here, the rules of priority need to be considered. The general rule of priority is that 'any vehicle crossing the path of another must give way'.

- If you were turning left from the minor road, you must give way to any traffic on the major road, but a vehicle turning in the same direction as you from the road opposite should give way to you. You must take care however, as they may attempt to force their way out before you. Make sure you watch them, and be prepared to wait if it looks as if they are going to proceed.

- If you are turning right from the minor road and a car opposite is going straight ahead, then you must give way to all traffic on the major road and the vehicle opposite, as you would be crossing in front of it.

- If you are going straight ahead, then you have priority over traffic opposite you, but you must still give way to traffic on the major road.

The most difficult situation is when you are turning right and a vehicle opposite is turning to their right, that is, you are going in opposite directions. Neither of you has priority, as you are both crossing each other's path.

- In this case, you need to make eye contact with the other driver and decide between you who is going to go first. Look for the tell-tale signs: a driver looking to their left and right, but avoiding looking at you, is almost certainly going to try to get out before you, while a driver who has stopped short of the line and is looking directly at you is probably going to let you go first. Look out for any signals they may give inviting you to go first, such as a wave or flashed lights.

> **TIP**
> Remember, flashed lights are only to attract your attention – it is what you see when you look at them that will tell you what the driver is trying to say.

If someone does wave you on, make sure it is safe first. Never trust anyone else to make that decision for you. The driver is only saying 'I'm letting you go first' – they are not saying that it is safe for you to go.

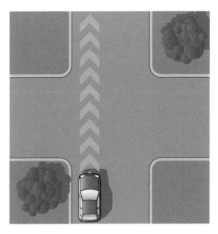

Special care is required at unmarked crossroads, where no one has priority

UNMARKED CROSSROADS

You may come to crossroads that have no road markings at all, particularly in housing estates or country lanes.

These require special care as no one has priority in any direction. Always approach these as if they were a totally blind junction: slow right down, stopping if necessary where the line would be, and make careful observations to your Right, Left, Ahead and Right again.

LIGHT-CONTROLLED CROSSROADS

Crossroads controlled by traffic lights are generally much easier to negotiate. Use the MSM/PSL routine as you approach and obey the traffic lights. Look out for filter arrows on the lights. These filter arrows turn green when there is no opposing traffic, allowing you to make your turn without struggling to find a safe gap. Of course, there is always the danger that someone is going to jump the lights, so careful observation is still needed.

If you are turning right and have to wait for a gap in the oncoming traffic, move forward to your turning point and wait for a suitable gap. If the lights turn red while you are still waiting, allow the last oncoming vehicle to pass and then make your turn. It is important that you clear the junction. Don't worry too much about traffic from the sides, as there will be some delay before their lights turn green; you should have plenty of time to get clear.

> **TIP**
> Remember the meanings of the lights:
> Green – go if it is safe to do so
> Amber – stop, unless to do so would cause an accident
> Red – stop behind the line
> Red and amber – stop and wait for the green light

The traffic light sequence in the UK goes green–amber–red–red/amber–green; in some other countries, including Ireland, the red/amber phase may be curtailed or missing all together

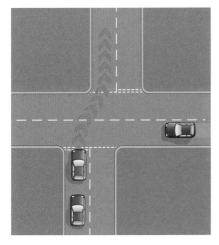 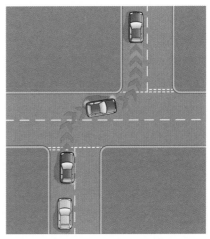

Going straight ahead at a slightly staggered crossroads (left); going straight ahead at a severely staggered crossroads should be treated as two turns: right and then left (right)

STAGGERED CROSSROADS

You will normally treat staggered crossroads in the same way as any other crossroads. At a staggered junction the minor road does not run straight across the main road, and the distance between the two parts of the minor road – the degree of 'stagger' – affects how you deal with it.

If you are on the minor road and intend to follow the road ahead, you need to assess the distance between the two staggered roads. If the stagger is less than two car lengths, you will not normally need to signal. Further apart than this, and you should treat it as two separate turns. The reason for this is that a following vehicle may not see the road ahead and may wonder what you intend to do.

YELLOW BOX JUNCTIONS

At busy crossroads and some other junctions, you may find yellow box markings on the road – like the diagram below.

- You must not enter the box unless your exit is clear.
- If traffic is tailed back and prevents you from driving through the yellow box, you must wait on your side of the box until the tailed-back traffic has moved on enough for you to exit the box.
- If you are turning right at a yellow box junction, you may wait inside the box for a suitable gap in the oncoming traffic, but only if your exit road is clear.

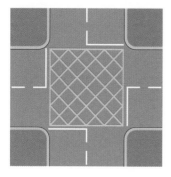

SUMMARY

Use the MSM/PSL routine as you approach. The golden rule for negotiating crossroads safely is to slow down enough so that you can stop if you need to, and make sure you look systematically into every road before proceeding.

Practice plan

First steps

Begin by going straight ahead on the major road, making sure you start the MSM routine as soon as you spot the sign or the actual crossroads. Then move on to turning from the major road into a minor road. Left turns are the easiest to start with, then progress to right turns. Don't forget to make the extra observation into the road opposite the one you are taking.

Gaining confidence

Practise turning from the minor road on to the major road, first to the left, then going straight ahead, and then to the right. Gradually work your way up from very quiet areas to more busy areas – but for now, avoid peak traffic periods. As you become more confident, try turning from major into minor roads in very busy areas. Take care with your positioning when turning right, so that you allow room for vehicles to pass on your left if possible, and that you don't give any misleading signals by stopping short of your turning point.

Ready for the test

Make sure you practise at any staggered, light-controlled and unmarked crossroads you can find. In particular, practise turning right at light-controlled crossroads where there is no filter arrow (the examiner's favourite). Practise other crossroads in busy traffic and at peak times.

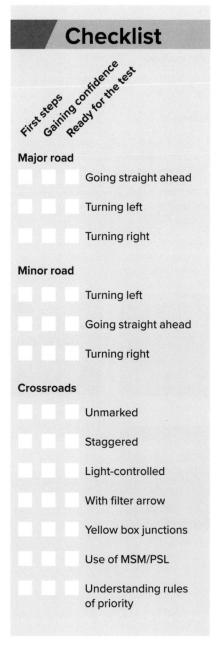

Checklist

First steps	Gaining confidence	Ready for the test	
			Major road
☐	☐	☐	Going straight ahead
☐	☐	☐	Turning left
☐	☐	☐	Turning right
			Minor road
☐	☐	☐	Turning left
☐	☐	☐	Going straight ahead
☐	☐	☐	Turning right
			Crossroads
☐	☐	☐	Unmarked
☐	☐	☐	Staggered
☐	☐	☐	Light-controlled
☐	☐	☐	With filter arrow
☐	☐	☐	Yellow box junctions
☐	☐	☐	Use of MSM/PSL
☐	☐	☐	Understanding rules of priority

1

All crossroads must be approached with caution.

Match actions 1, 2 and 3 listed below with these diagrams

Actions

1 Approach with caution, look well ahead and be prepared to stop. Remember other drivers may assume they have priority.

2 Look well ahead, slow down and be prepared to give way to traffic on the major road.

3 Look well ahead and into the side roads for approaching vehicles. Remember other drivers may not give you priority.

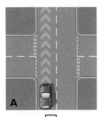

Answer ☐

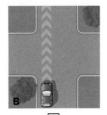

Answer ☐

Answer ☐

2

Traffic lights have three lights, red, amber, and green, which change from one to the other in a set order.

Number the boxes 1 to 5 to show the correct order.

☐ Amber ☐ Red ☐ Red and amber
☐ Red ☐ Green

3

What do the colours of traffic lights mean?

Fill in the correct colour for each of the following

1 Go ahead if the way is clear.

Colour _____

2 Stop and wait.

Colour _____

3 Stop unless you have crossed the stop line or you are so close to it that stopping might cause an accident.

Colour _____

4 Stop and wait at the stop line.

Colour _____

4

Some traffic lights have green filters. Do they mean...

1 You can filter in the direction of the arrow only when the main light is showing green?

2 You can filter even when the main light is not showing green?

Answer ☐

5

At some traffic lights and junctions you will see yellow criss-cross lines (box junctions). Can you...

Tick the correct boxes

	YES	NO
1 Wait within them when going ahead if your exit is not clear?	☐	☐
2 Wait within them when going right if your exit is not clear?	☐	☐
3 Wait within them if there is oncoming traffic stopping you turning right but your exit is clear?	☐	☐

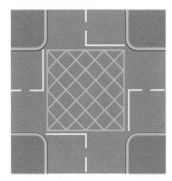

6

The diagram shows two vehicles, travelling in opposite directions, turning right at a crossroads.
Are these statements true or false?

Tick the appropriate boxes

	True	False
1 The safest route is to pass each other offside to offside.	☐	☐
2 If the approaching vehicle flashes its headlamps, I should turn as quickly as possible.	☐	☐
3 I should always try to get eye-to-eye contact with the driver of the other vehicle to determine which course to take.	☐	☐

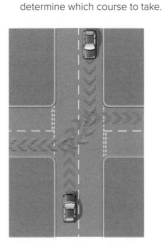

ROUNDABOUTS

You must show that you can negotiate roundabouts safely and smoothly. You should approach at a safe speed, taking up the appropriate position on the road and indicating correctly. You should join the roundabout smoothly and with due consideration for other road users, taking the correct course around the roundabout and leaving at the appropriate exit.

How to do it

As always, use the MSM/PSL routine to help you to negotiate roundabouts.

As you approach the roundabout you will normally see a large map sign showing where the various roads go. This sign will be positioned far enough away so that you will have time to read it, select your route and take up the appropriate position in the road well before you reach the roundabout itself.

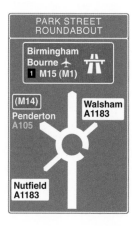

Whether in a lesson, practising, or on your test, you'll be told which direction and the exit number to take, and sometimes the destination shown on the signs.

The details of exactly what you should do depend entirely on the direction you intend to take, so we will deal with each option in turn.

> **LEGAL REQUIREMENTS**
> See *The Highway Code*, rules 184–190 for dealing with roundabouts.

There are, however, some general rules that you should follow:
- Take note of and act appropriately on all the information shown as you approach the roundabout, including traffic lights, road markings and signs.
- Always give priority to any traffic approaching from your right.
- You must go around the roundabout – this is particularly important at mini-roundabouts, where you must drive around the central marking.
- Watch out for pedestrians crossing near the roundabout, traffic crossing in front of you, vehicles that are signalling incorrectly or badly positioned, and cyclists, horse-riders or large vehicles, which may take a different course.

TAKING THE FIRST EXIT
This is usually to the left but does not necessarily have to be.

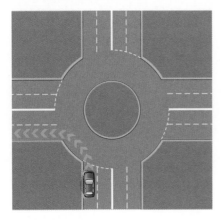

Taking the first exit

Approach
As soon as you can read the map sign, check your main and left mirrors and, if safe, signal left. Position yourself in the left-hand lane, and only then adjust your speed. Brake smoothly and progressively down to an appropriate speed.

As a guide, 20mph is a good average speed for a medium-sized roundabout with moderate traffic. If you can see that the roundabout is busy or smaller than normal, you should approach more slowly. You need to get to the appropriate speed when you are about six car lengths (around 20m) away from the roundabout.

At this point, select a lower gear, probably second or – if the roundabout is quiet – third. At this speed, you will have about five seconds to look and see if there is a safe gap in the traffic for you to enter the roundabout.

Observations
Remember you will need to look Right, Left and Right again. Make sure you look ahead to check that any vehicle in front of you has moved on, and that you are following the curve of the road and staying in your lane as you approach the line.

> **TIP**
> Bear in mind that you will tend to steer where you look. Take care not to drift out to the right as you look right.

In these last 20m, try to adjust your speed gently in order to slot into a safe gap. If the traffic is busy, try to anticipate gaps by looking for 'blockers'. Blockers are vehicles (the bigger the better) turning into the road you are leaving, and preferably spotted as they come around the roundabout. As they exit the roundabout they will block any traffic from the right, creating a gap which may be big enough to enable you to go.

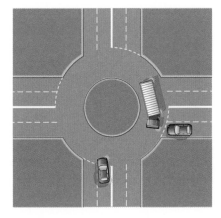

The red car is acting on the movement of the lorry, which is an effective 'blocker'

Try to keep moving as smoothly as possible by adjusting your speed sooner, rather than at the last moment. If you slow down too much you will need a much bigger gap to enable you to get back up to speed. Too fast, and you won't have time to look properly and may not be able to judge the gap quickly enough, forcing you to stop.

TIP
Roundabouts are designed to allow traffic to flow smoothly. Try to keep moving, no matter how slowly, if at all possible.

Leaving the roundabout
Keep well to the left of the roundabout, following the outside edge of the road. As you approach your exit, check your left mirror again and make sure your left signal is still on. Position yourself so that you follow the curve of the road, and try to maintain a steady speed as you exit. Remember that there may be sharp bends as you leave the roundabout. Look ahead into the new road to spot any immediate hazards, and check your main and right mirrors before accelerating away.

TURNING RIGHT

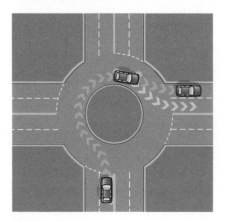

Turning right

Approach

A right turn is any road which is to the right of '12 o'clock', as shown on the map sign (see the example on page 119). Note that the layout of the road may not exactly match the sign – road designers sometimes distort the map to make sure traffic takes a preferred route.

When you are close enough to read the map sign, check your main and right mirrors and signal right. As soon as it is safe to do so, position yourself into the right-hand lane, or right-hand side of your road, before adjusting your speed, slowing to 20mph as before. Look for a safe gap and join the roundabout, staying in the right lane close to the central island. Try to maintain a steady speed as you circle the roundabout.

Count the exits off as you pass them. On your test, you will be told the exit number and the examiner may count for you. Remember to count only the exit roads, not those that enter the roundabout.

Leaving the roundabout

As you pass the exit before the road you want to take, check your left mirror to make sure there isn't a vehicle on the inside, and signal left to show you are leaving at the next exit.

> **TIP**
> If there is something to your left, keep your right signal on and continue for a full turn around the roundabout until you again reach the exit you want.

Maintain your position to the right and keep a steady speed until you are pointing at the exit you are taking. Check your left mirror for vehicles on your inside and, if safe, steer to exit into the left-hand side or lane of the new road.

> **TIP**
> Keeping a steady speed helps other road users to predict your course. If you keep changing your speed it may confuse them.

TAKING ANY OTHER EXIT

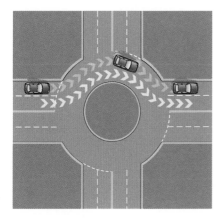

*Taking the second exit –
or straight ahead*

Approach

As soon as you can read the map sign begin the MSM/PSL routine. Check your mirrors but normally you do not signal. Position yourself in the left-hand lane, reduce your speed to 20mph and select the appropriate gear. If the left-hand lane is busy you may use the middle of three lanes, but take extra care when exiting as there may be traffic on your left. Look to find a gap, adjusting your speed as necessary. When it is safe, join the roundabout, staying in your lane on the roundabout itself.

Leaving the roundabout

As you pass the exit before the one you want, check your mirrors and signal left to show you intend to take the next exit. Maintain your position and keep a steady speed.

Look into the new road and check your mirror again, remembering to take special care if you have chosen to use the middle lane. Exit into the left-hand lane if possible and have another check in your main and right mirrors before accelerating away.

If you used the middle lane and there is traffic to your left, you may have to exit into the right-hand lane of the new road. If this happens, make sure you accelerate briskly to prevent cars from passing on your left, and get back into the left lane as soon as it is safe.

ROUNDABOUTS WITH LANE MARKINGS

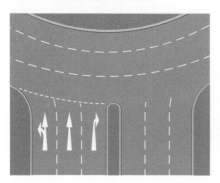

MULTIPLE ROUNDABOUTS

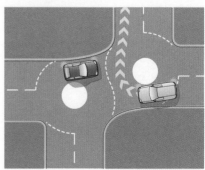

Many roundabouts, particularly the larger ones, have markings or signs to indicate which lane you should take for your destination. These markings over-ride the rules given previously.

Look for arrows in the lanes or road signs as you approach the roundabout. When you have a choice of lanes for the same direction it is usually better to choose the left-hand option, as it is likely to be easier as you exit the roundabout.

Some roundabouts now have spiral-type markings. Traffic turning right merely has to stay in lane and follow the lane as it 'spirals' out to the outside edge at the desired exit. The basic rule at these roundabouts is to make sure that you stay centrally within the lane markings.

You may come across multiple roundabouts or a series of connected roundabouts. These should always be treated separately: take each roundabout in turn, and always give priority to traffic on your right.

TRAFFIC LIGHTS

The use of traffic lights at roundabouts means that many roundabouts are actually a series of light-controlled junctions. Look out for vehicles 'jumping the lights' or failing to move on green. However, from the learner's point of view, these junctions are easier to negotiate than ordinary roundabouts as you generally don't have to worry about finding a suitable gap.

ROUNDABOUTS: SUMMARY			
APPROACHING	**First Exit**	**Right**	**Straight/ Intermediate**
Mirrors	main and left	main and right	main
Signal	left	right	nothing
Position	left lane	right lane	left unless busy, then middle
Speed	20mph or less	20mph or less	20mph or less
Look	RLR again minimum	RLR again minimum	RLR again minimum
LEAVING			
Mirrors	left	left	left
Signal	left still on	left as you pass exit before the one you want	left as you pass exit before the one you want
Position	left lane	left or right lane	left or right lane
Speed	maintain a steady speed	maintain a steady speed	maintain a steady speed
Look	left and ahead	left and ahead	left and ahead

TIP

Be careful at roundabouts where destinations are marked for each lane. Make sure you are in the correct lane for your destination.

CYCLISTS AND HORSE RIDERS

It's worth noting that these road users can stay in the left lane on a roundabout while signalling right as they pass an exit, to indicate that they are carrying on round. This is different to car drivers, so you should be careful when you come across these groups at a roundabout.

Practice plan

First steps

It may be helpful to practise slowing down and changing gear on an empty, straight road before practising roundabouts. Practise slowing to 20mph, 10mph, walking speed (about 4mph) and coming to a complete stop, each time selecting the appropriate gear and driving off again. Make sure there is no one behind you.

You might also try standing near a roundabout, to watch how other drivers slot into gaps. This will give you a feel for the size of gap and speed you will need. You will also see how often others indicate wrongly or take the wrong lane; this should make you more vigilant when you use roundabouts.

Try to pay attention when you are a passenger. Ask yourself if you would take that gap.

Begin by negotiating medium-size, but quiet, roundabouts. Some industrial estates or suburban areas may have suitable roundabouts for your early practice sessions. Try to pick a quiet time, avoiding rush hour or the school run.

Begin by taking the first exit, aiming for a steady speed and accurate steering. Make sure you use the MSM/PSL routine, starting it as soon as possible and following through all the stages.

Next, try taking the right turn – preferably the last exit. Remember to be particularly aware of vehicles on your left, and concentrate on your speed and position when leaving. If the worst comes to the worst, go around again.

Finally, practise taking intermediate exits – second left or straight ahead. Again, concentrate on using the MSM/PSL routine correctly.

Gaining confidence

When you are happy with moderate conditions, practise on busier roundabouts and mini-roundabouts. Remember to listen to your supervisor – their judgement of suitable gaps will be more developed, so be prepared to stop or go as they instruct you.

Practise judging the gaps. You could try saying aloud whether you would 'go' or 'wait', and ask your supervisor to confirm your decision before proceeding.

Ready for the test

Choose a quiet time of day to practise on larger roundabouts. Include roundabouts with lane markings, traffic lights and multiple roundabouts. Aim to keep moving if at all possible, and try to spot suitable gaps earlier. Aim to be fluent and smooth in both your use of speed and steering.

Checklist

First steps
Gaining confidence
Ready for the test

- Start MSM/PSL when you can read the sign
- Select appropriate lane or position
- Use appropriate speed/gear for the conditions.
- Make effective observations
- Steer accurately
- Keep a steady speed
- Use of mirrors
- Signals timed accurately
- Exiting smoothly and safely

1

Which of the following statements describes the correct procedure when approaching a roundabout?

Put letter A, B or C in the box

A The broken white line at a roundabout means I must stop and give way to traffic already on the roundabout.

B The broken white line at a roundabout means I must give priority to traffic already on the roundabout.

C The broken white line means I should give way to any traffic approaching from my immediate right.

Answer ☐

2

The following sentences give guidance on lane discipline on a roundabout.

Fill in the missing words

1 When turning left at a roundabout, I should stay in the ___ ___ ___ ___ hand lane and should stay in that lane throughout.

2 When going ahead at a roundabout, I should be in the ___ ___ ___ ___ hand lane, and should stay in that lane throughout, unless conditions dictate otherwise.

3 When turning right at a roundabout, I should approach in the r___ ___ ___ ___ hand lane, or approach as if turning right at a junction, and stay in that lane throughout.

3

Cyclists are particularly vulnerable at roundabouts. Why might this be?

Answer _____

_____

_____

4

The letters A, B and C in the diagram mark places where you should signal.

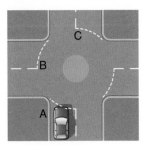

Complete the sentences

1 I would signal at **A** when turning __ __ __ __.

2 I would signal at **B** when g__ __ __ __ __ __ __ __ __.

3 I would signal at **A** and at **C** when turning __ __ __ __ __.

5

At a roundabout you should always use a safe routine.

Fill in the missing words

M__ __ __ __ __ __ __, s __ __ __ __ __ __,
p__ __ __ __ __ __ __ __, s__ __ __ __ __,
l__ __ __.

6

What does this sign mean?

Write 1, 2 or 3 in the box

1 Roundabout

2 Mini-roundabout

3 Vehicles may pass either side.

Answer ☐

STARTING ON A HILL AND AT AN ANGLE

Several times during the Driving Test, candidates will be asked to pull over and park on the left. Some of these stops are to give instructions for specific manoeuvres or exercises, while others are just to see how efficiently the candidate selects a safe place and then moves away. You may be asked to stop close behind a parked car, or on a hill, or both. You need to be able to move away safely and under full control. If on a hill, you must not roll backwards. If behind a parked car, you must pull away only when it is safe to do so and without getting too close to the parked car.

How to do it

In Section 2, we dealt with moving away and stopping normally on a road with no gradient. When moving away on a hill or at an angle (from behind a parked car) we need to modify the POM or preparation–observation–manoeuvre routine slightly.

> **LEGAL REQUIREMENTS**
> Rule 159 of *The Highway Code* has general instructions for moving away

MOVING OFF FACING UPHILL

By now you will probably be carrying out the moving away procedure quite routinely and with some confidence. The routine for moving away when facing uphill is almost the same, except that you need to use more gas to overcome the gradient, and a firmer biting point to avoid rolling backwards.

Preparation

Press the clutch pedal all the way down and select first gear.

Set your gas by gently squeezing the accelerator pedal down. Because gravity is going to use up some of the power, in order to get up the hill you will need to use a bit more gas than on the flat. For a slight gradient, use about a third as much again as on the flat, and for a very steep hill, double your revs. If, for example, you normally set your revs to 1,500rpm on the flat, you would need around 2,000rpm on a slight hill and 3,000rpm on a very steep hill. Obviously, a moderately steep hill would be somewhere in between these two, at around 2,500rpm.

Having set your gas higher than normal, it is important that you don't hold biting point for too long, as to do so could burn out the clutch mechanism. So before finding biting point, have a quick look to see if you are likely to get an opportunity to go soon.

When you think there is a safe gap coming, find biting point. Remember, gravity is going to try to make you roll downhill – in this case backwards – so make sure you have a firm biting point. As on the flat, you will hear the engine revs drop as you reach biting point and the nose of the car will rise a little bit. Bring the clutch up one or two millimetres higher than normal, so that the nose rises as far as it will go without the engine stalling.

Observation

Look all round the car using all your mirrors, and finish by checking your right blind spot. If it is safe, begin your manoeuvre.

TIP

If it is not safe and you cannot see a safe gap coming in the next few seconds, release the gas pedal and press down the clutch below biting point again while you wait. This prevents excessive wear on the clutch, overheating or burning. When you see a safe gap approaching, start the preparation phase again.

Manoeuvre

Release the handbrake and hold your feet still. The car will move forwards smoothly. Because you are going uphill and revving the engine faster, it will take a little longer for the wheels to catch up to the speed of the engine, so make sure you keep your feet still a little longer than normal. Wait until you feel the engine smooth out before 'pedalling', bringing the clutch up smoothly at the same time as you gently squeeze the gas pedal down.

TIP

On a level road, if you need to get away quite quickly – for example, when emerging directly onto a 50mph or 60mph road – use the uphill start procedure.

Remember, when you are going uphill you need to let the engine rev a little faster than normal before you change gear – when you come off the gas and depress the clutch, gravity will slow the car down much more than on the flat.

MOVING OFF FACING DOWNHILL

If you are facing downhill and release the handbrake, the car will roll forwards, in the direction you want to go – but outside your control. Because of this, the routine is slightly different.

Preparation

Press the clutch fully down and select first gear. On steep hills, you may find it easier to start off in second gear rather than first. Because of the gradient, you will quickly reach the speed at which you would normally change into second. Press down firmly on the footbrake and release the handbrake. The car should still be stationary.

Observation

Make all-round observation, using all mirrors and finishing by checking your right blind spot.

The warning sign for steep hill downwards

Manoeuvre

If it is safe, release the footbrake and smoothly bring the clutch all the way up as the car starts to roll forward. At the same time, move your right foot to the gas pedal and gently squeeze. Try to perform these movements fluently and smoothly, without either rushing or moving too slowly. The whole procedure should feel very similar to a gear change and take about the same time to perform. Practise this a few times on a flat road first, with the engine off, just to get a feel for the timing.

MOVING AWAY AT AN ANGLE

When moving away from behind a parked car, you need to be careful to allow enough clearance space around the obstruction. This will naturally cause you to pull out much further into the road than you would do normally. Couple this with the fact that your view of the road ahead will be limited by the parked car itself, and you significantly increase the risk of an incident.

Use the same basic procedure – preparation–observation–manoeuvre – but this time you need to greatly increase the observation and keep a slower speed until you are clear of the parked car.

Preparation

Your preparation should be exactly the same as normal: press the clutch down fully and select first gear. Set a little gas and find biting point.

Observation

Carry out all-round observations as normal, but you must now be very careful of potential hazards hidden by the parked car. These might include pedestrians, another vehicle moving off at the same time, and traffic emerging from a junction on the left just ahead of the parked car. Make sure you finish your first observations by checking your blind spots carefully: you will be coming out more slowly than normal and will therefore need a much bigger gap. If your view is very restricted, you should signal right in case there is a vehicle approaching that you are unable to see. However, if you can see a vehicle approaching, delay the signal until it has passed – a signal just as the driver is about to reach you may cause them to panic.

TIP

If you can see the rear tyres of the car in front, then you have enough room to steer out without reversing first.

Manoeuvre

When you are sure it is safe, release the handbrake, keep your feet still and steer briskly to the right.

Immediately check your blind spot again. When looking forwards, you will probably need to lean to your right to be able to see past the obstruction and the pillar of your windscreen.

Instead of pedalling normally, you will now keep the car moving slowly by using clutch control. Keep looking up and down the road, using right blind-spot checks or mirrors as the angle dictates.

When you are sure that you are clear of the parked car, steer briskly left to get straight in the road, and then straighten your steering wheel. Have one more look behind you, using the main mirror now, and double-check the area in front of the obstruction to see if it is safe to accelerate away.

If it is safe, bring the clutch up all the way and at the same time gently squeeze the gas pedal to accelerate smoothly away.

> **TIP**
>
> If you are manoeuvring downhill very slowly, control the brake in exactly the same way as you control the clutch — with tiny movements of the pedal.

Remember, because you are pulling out very slowly and have a limited view, it is much more likely that another vehicle will close up on you as you emerge. Be prepared to stop at any time and allow traffic to pass.

Practice plan

First steps
Practise uphill starts on slight gradients and gradually work your way onto steeper hills.

On a flat road and with the engine turned off, practise the procedure for the downhill start. Aim to be fluent and smooth, taking the same amount of time as it takes you to change gear normally to complete the movements. When you are comfortable with the movements, use the engine and move on to downhill slopes.

Practise moving away from behind a builder's skip or parked trailer. Stop well back at first until you are confident in your control.

Gaining confidence
Practise uphill starts on steeper hills and in busier areas.

Practise downhill starts on gradually steeper gradients and in busier traffic. Try to find some very steep hills where you could move off in second gear.

Practise moving away at an angle from behind other vehicles. Gradually get closer to the obstruction until you can move away in one quarter of your car's length. This should be your minimum distance.

Ready for the test
By now you should be confident when moving away on hills or at an angle. Combine the two by practising moving away from behind a parked car on a hill.

Checklist

First steps Gaining confidence Ready for the test

POM routine

Uphill

- ☐ ☐ ☐ Setting enough gas
- ☐ ☐ ☐ Finding a high enough biting point
- ☐ ☐ ☐ Not rolling backwards

Downhill

- ☐ ☐ ☐ Use of footbrake
- ☐ ☐ ☐ Smooth movement from footbrake to gas
- ☐ ☐ ☐ Smooth use of clutch
- ☐ ☐ ☐ Appropriate choice of gear

First steps Gaining confidence Ready for the test

Angle

- ☐ ☐ ☐ Thorough observations
- ☐ ☐ ☐ Maximising the view ahead
- ☐ ☐ ☐ Clutch control
- ☐ ☐ ☐ Accurate steering
- ☐ ☐ ☐ Adequate clearance
- ☐ ☐ ☐ Maintaining slow speed until clear

1

Are these statements about moving off at an angle true or false?

Tick the appropriate boxes   **True**   **False**

1 I should check my mirrors as I am pulling out. ☐ ☐

2 I should check my mirrors and blindspot before I pull out. ☐ ☐

3 I should move out as quickly as possible. ☐ ☐

4 The amount of steering required will depend on how close I am to the vehicle in front. ☐ ☐

5 I should look for oncoming traffic. ☐ ☐

6 As long as I am signalling, people will know what I am doing. I will be able to pull out because somebody will let me in. ☐ ☐

2

Are these statements about moving off uphill true or false?

Tick the appropriate boxes   **True**   **False**

1 On an uphill gradient the car will tend to roll back. ☐ ☐

2 To stop the car rolling back I need to use more acceleration. ☐ ☐

3 I do not need to use the handbrake. ☐ ☐

4 The biting point may be slightly higher. ☐ ☐

5 I need to press the accelerator pedal further down than when moving off on the level. ☐ ☐

6 I need to allow more time to pull away. ☐ ☐

7 The main controls I use will be the clutch pedal, the accelerator pedal and the handbrake. ☐ ☐

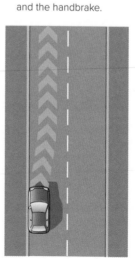

3

Are these statements about moving off downhill true or false?

Tick the appropriate boxes

	True	False
1 The car will tend to roll forwards.	☐	☐
2 The main controls I use will be the handbrake, the clutch pedal and the accelerator pedal.	☐	☐
3 The only gear I can move off in is 1st gear.	☐	☐
4 I should release the handbrake while keeping the foot-brake applied.	☐	☐
5 I should look round just before moving off.	☐	☐
6 I must not have my foot on the foot-brake as I start to release the clutch.	☐	☐

4

The following statements are about approaching a junction when going uphill or downhill. With which do you agree?

When going downhill ...	YES	NO
1 It is more difficult to slow down	☐	☐
2 Putting the clutch down will help slow the car down	☐	☐
3 The higher the gear, the greater the control	☐	☐
4 When changing gear you may need to use the foot-brake at the same time as the clutch	☐	☐

When going uphill ...	YES	NO
5 Early use of mirrors, signals, brakes, gears and steering will help to position the car correctly	☐	☐
6 You may need to use your handbrake more often	☐	☐
7 When you change gear, the car tends to slow down	☐	☐

OTHER TYPES OF ROADS

You need to be able to drive safely on any type of road. So far we have mainly concerned ourselves with ordinary single carriageway roads. In this section, we shall look at how you must modify your driving on dual carriageways, single track roads and one-way roads.

How to do it

DUAL CARRIAGEWAYS

A dual carriageway consists of two separate roads, usually running parallel, divided by a physical barrier or central reservation. There are normally two lanes on each carriageway or road, but this can vary. If the carriageway has only one lane, it is still classed as a dual carriageway if there is a barrier or reservation to divide it from traffic on the other side. The main advantage of dual carriageways is that traffic can travel faster, as there is no threat from oncoming vehicles. Because of these faster speeds, you must leave a longer gap between you and the vehicle in front. For full information on how to judge the correct space to leave, including the 'Two-second Rule', see Section 17.

There are three main elements to using dual carriageways: joining, travelling on the dual carriageway, and leaving.

LEGAL REQUIREMENTS

The Highway Code deals with items related to dual carriageways in rules 130–134 and 137–139, single track roads in rules 155–156 and one-way streets in rule 143.

Joining

You may join a dual carriageway from a slip road or acceleration lane. The purpose of this stretch of road is to allow you to build up your speed to match that of the traffic on the dual carriageway. As you get on to the acceleration lane, accelerate and work your way up through the gears. There will be some kind of physical barrier between the slip road and the main carriageway, such as a raised grass verge. As you see the end of this barrier, you should begin the MSM/PSL routine.

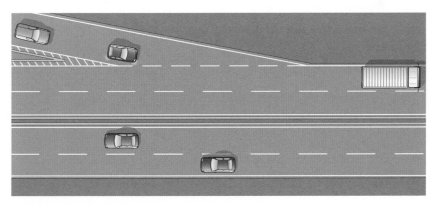

Joining a dual carriageway from a slip road

Mirrors

Check the main mirror for following traffic and the right mirror to see if any vehicle is attempting to overtake you.

Signal

Indicate right as you pass the end of the barrier to show traffic on the main carriageway that you intend to join. This is essential, as many 'on-slips' also double as 'off-slips', so there may be traffic attempting to join the slip road from the main carriageway, or other road users may think you are going straight off again.

Position

Maintain your normal road position – or, if it is safe, you may move over towards the right-hand side of the slip road.

Speed

Adjust your speed to match that of the traffic already on the main carriageway. To avoid travelling abreast of a vehicle on the main carriageway, either accelerate or slow down slightly.

Look

Check your right mirror to look for a safe gap. When you are sure it is safe, glance to your right to double check. You must give priority to traffic on the main carriageway.

Only when you are 100% certain it is safe to do so, steer very slightly right to drift into the space in the left-hand lane of the dual carriageway. You must not cross the hatched or shaded area as you join, but must wait until there is a single broken line.

You should stay in the left-hand lane long enough to get used to the faster speed of the road – it can be difficult to judge the speed of traffic in your mirrors until you are acclimatised.

Most learner drivers worry that they will not be able to join the flow of traffic and will end up stopped at the end of the slip road. Provided that you make sure to match your speed to the speed of the traffic flow, this will not happen.

> **TIP**
> Remember, it is not the speed you are doing that is the problem, it is the difference in speed between you and others that creates a problem. Try to build up your speed before joining so that you can 'go with the flow'.

TRAVELLING ON
THE DUAL CARRIAGEWAY

It is essential that you look further ahead than normal because of the faster speeds. Most dual carriageways are relatively straight, so you should be able to see further with ease. Instead of just looking at the rear of the vehicle in front, look as far down the line of traffic as you can.

As a general rule, try to look at least half a mile ahead – at the top speed of 70mph that is just over 20 seconds away. Use scanning techniques to monitor the situation ahead and remember to make frequent use of your mirrors, so that you always know what is happening behind you as well.

Use the following as a guidance:

- You should travel in the left-hand lane, only using the outer lane to overtake, and return to the left-hand lane once the manoeuvre is complete. If you are overtaking a number of other vehicles, you may stay in the outer lanes until you have passed them all. Do not hold up faster-moving traffic by staying unnecessarily in an outer lane.
- Try to travel at the speed limit for your vehicle if it is safe to do so, overtaking slower traffic as necessary. Remember that for vehicles towing a trailer or caravan, coaches and lorries the speed limit is reduced to 60mph, or 50mph if the lorry is over 7.5 tonnes. As soon as you see this type of vehicle ahead start planning to overtake them, as they will almost certainly be going more slowly than you.

- Try to avoid using your brakes unless it proves necessary. Look out for brake lights in the distance and as soon as you see any, check your mirror and ease off the gas: you will find that, in most instances, you will avoid the need to brake.
- The stopping distance at 70mph is 96m, or 24 car lengths. You need to leave a much bigger gap than you may think. Keep repeating the 'Two-second Rule' as you drive. You may find that other vehicles will pull into the safe gap that you have created. Check your mirror and ease off the gas slightly to re-establish it.
- Look out for roads joining or leaving the main carriageway. As you approach a slip road, check your mirrors to see if there will be a gap in the next lane. If you see a vehicle trying to join the carriageway and it is safe for you to do so, move out into the next lane to create a gap for them. If you cannot move out, slow down slightly to create a space in front of you.
- When approaching an exit or 'off-slip' be especially wary of vehicles cutting across your path at the last moment.

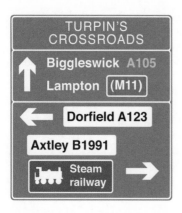

LEAVING

Look out for signs warning you that your exit is coming up. These are usually well in advance of the exit. If you are overtaking at the time you see the sign, you will need to get back into the left-hand lane. As you get closer to the exit slip road, you may see countdown boards at intervals of about 100m. At the first countdown board before your exit, begin the MSM/PSL routine. Where there are no countdown markers plan well ahead to give yourself sufficient time to begin the MSM/PSL routine.

Mirrors
Check the main and left mirrors.

Signal
Indicate left to show that you intend to leave the main carriageway.

Position
At the start of the slip road, check your left door mirror again and steer gently left into the slip road.

Speed
Only when you are in the slip road should you slow down. Keep an eye on your speedometer to make sure you are slowing down enough – because you have become used to the faster speed on the dual carriageway, it will appear that you are going much slower than you actually are.

Look
Look ahead for the next junction, paying particular attention to vehicles in front that may slow down suddenly.

After leaving a dual carriageway you must be very careful with your speed. It will take several minutes for your speed perception to readjust to the slower speeds and you may be going much faster than you think.

Countdown markers warn you when you are approaching a major junction on a dual carriageway

This sign warns that the dual carriageway is about revert to single carriageway

SINGLE-TRACK ROADS

These are roads that are not wide enough for two vehicles to pass at once. They are usually found in rural areas where there may also be high hedges and tight bends, so extra care is needed. Remember the golden rule for speed (see page 195) and slow down when your view ahead is limited.

Most single-track roads have marked passing places. When you see another vehicle coming towards you, continue onwards until there is only one passing place left between you. The first vehicle to reach this passing place must stop and pull well into the left to allow the other vehicle to pass. If you can see that you are both approaching passing places either side of a stretch of road, slow down enough to be able to stop and pull into the one nearest to you and wait for the other vehicle to pass.

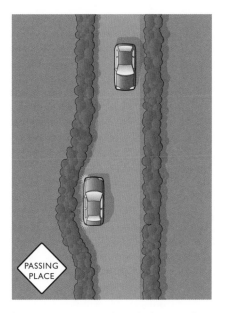

It is courteous to acknowledge another driver who has pulled over to let you pass on a single-track road

- Use the passing places to allow following traffic to overtake you. Be considerate to drivers of large vehicles and traffic coming uphill – let them through whenever you can. Never park in a passing place.
- Do not try to keep in to your left, but rather drive in the middle of the road so that you can see and be seen more easily.
- Take care when visibility is limited by high hedges or tight bends: use your horn to warn other road users of your presence. At night you can use flashed lights to give a similar warning.

ONE-WAY ROADS

You must travel in the direction shown by the blue-and-white signs. Look out for contra-flow lanes for cyclists or buses. Other than these, you should not have to worry about oncoming traffic, although driving the wrong way down a one-way street is a surprisingly common mistake, especially in areas popular with tourists.

- Drive in the most appropriate lane for the direction you intend to take at the end of the one-way system: use the left-hand lane if you intend to go left or straight on, and the right-hand lane if you intend to turn right.
- When turning right off a one-way street, position your car well to the right as soon as possible.
- It is permissible to overtake on the left, so take care, as traffic could be passing you on either side.
- You must not reverse in a one-way road other than to manoeuvre normally. It is an offence to reverse any further than necessary, so you may not reverse through a one-way section to effect a short-cut.
- Look out for signs indicating the end of a one-way system and make sure you return to the correct side of the road.

MOTORWAYS

Learner drivers are allowed onto motorways, as long as they are driving a car with dual controls and are accompanied by a professional driving instructor. These are voluntary lessons and you will not be asked to drive on a motorway as part of the Driving Test. See Section 24 for more information on motorway driving.

Practice plan

First steps

Try to find a relatively quiet period to practise joining and leaving a dual carriageway for the first time. Practise accelerating to an appropriate speed when joining, and slowing down effectively when leaving the main carriageway. If you intend to follow a section of dual carriageway by leaving and coming straight back on again, take care at the roundabouts or junctions as you leave: the designers were not expecting people to do this and it can be difficult to get into the appropriate lane.

Practise using one-way streets. Pay particular attention to the signs and markings and make sure you know what they all mean.

Gaining confidence

Practise joining and leaving dual carriageways, and stay on long enough to practise overtaking. If there is a location where you can join at a T-junction, make sure you practise that.

If you have any single-track roads in your area, practise using passing places. Try to practise any sections with tight bends, remembering to warn others of your presence when you cannot see very far ahead.

Practise longer one-way systems, which are often found in town centres. Look out for signs and markings indicating the use of lanes.

Ready for the test

You should be confident about joining and leaving the dual carriageway by now. Try to find junctions where the slip roads are either unusually short or long. Make sure you practise interchanges between two dual carriageways if possible.

Make sure you are familiar with any one-way systems in your area. Practise driving through gyratory systems (huge roundabouts that are really one way systems with traffic lights and lanes) if there are any near you.

Checklist

First steps *Gaining confidence* *Ready for the test*

Dual carriageways

☐ ☐ ☐ Joining – acceleration, MSM/PSL

☐ ☐ ☐ On – speed, lane discipline, overtaking, safe gap

☐ ☐ ☐ Leaving – MSM/PSL, speed

Single-track roads

☐ ☐ ☐ Positioning

☐ ☐ ☐ Passing places

☐ ☐ ☐ Use of horn/lights

☐ ☐ ☐ Speed

One-way systems

☐ ☐ ☐ Seeing the signs

☐ ☐ ☐ Lane discipline

☐ ☐ ☐ Turning right

1

Which of these signs means one-way traffic?

A   B

Answer ☐

2

Are these statements about one-way systems true or false?

Tick the correct boxes	True	False
1 In one-way streets traffic can pass me on both sides.	☐	☐
2 Roundabouts are one-way systems.	☐	☐
3 For normal driving I should stay on the left.	☐	☐
4 I should look out for road markings and get in lane early.	☐	☐

3

What do these signs mean?

A

Answer _____

B

Answer _____

C

Answer _____

4

Which of the signs above would you expect to see on a dual carriageway?

Answer _____
_____
_____
_____

5

Dual carriageways can appear similar to motorways, but there are important differences. Which of the following statements apply to dual carriageways?

Tick the relevant boxes

1 Reflective studs are not used. ☐

2 Cyclists are allowed. ☐

3 The speed limit is always 60mph. ☐

4 You cannot turn right to enter or leave a dual carriageway. ☐

5 Milk floats and slow moving farm vehicles are prohibited. ☐

6

When travelling at 70mph on a dual carriageway, which lane would you use?

Answer _____

7

When turning right from a minor road on to a dual carriageway, where would you wait...

A When there is a wide central reserve?
Answer _____
_____
_____

B When the central reserve is too narrow for your car?
Answer _____
_____
_____

_____

8

Why is it important to plan your movements especially early when leaving a dual carriageway to the right (see diagram below)?

Answer _____
_____
_____
_____
_____

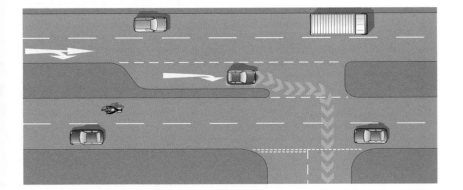

REVERSING

You need to be able to reverse your car in a straight line, and around a corner, either to the left or to the right. When reversing, you must keep your rear wheel reasonably close and parallel to the kerb. You must give way to any other road users and make sure that your observations are mainly to the rear of your vehicle, in the direction you are moving.

How to do it

REVERSING IN A STRAIGHT LINE

Find a suitable place to park on a straight, quiet road. Park a little further from the kerb than you would normally – your left wheels should be around 20–30cm from the kerb. Make sure that you are parallel to the kerb and that your wheels are straight.

Once you are safely parked, look over your left shoulder through the rear window. You will find it easier to see clearly if you move closer to your door and swivel your bottom in the seat so that your thighs are pointing 45° to the left, towards the gear lever. If you find it more comfortable, you can place your left hand on the back of the passenger's seat to help you turn around. If you choose to do this, then your right hand should hold the steering wheel at the top, in the '12 o'clock' position.

You are allowed to remove your seatbelt when you are reversing, which may make it more comfortable for you to turn around in your seat. However, you must make sure you put the seatbelt back on again before driving forwards.

TIP
If the seatbelt restricts your body movement when reversing, pull the chest belt out and slip your arm over it so that it goes under your armpit.

LEGAL REQUIREMENTS
You may only reverse as far as necessary and you MUST NOT reverse from a minor road into a major road. *The Highway Code* has a short section dedicated to reversing, which you will find in rules 200–203.

Look at the position of the kerb at the bottom edge of the rear window. There may be a sticker or head-restraint that will act as a reminder. You must remember the exact position of the kerb on the rear window, as this is your reference point to tell you when you are straight.

Preparation
Put the gear lever into reverse, set a little gas and find biting point. You will be moving very slowly using clutch control, so be careful not to bring the clutch pedal too high.

Observation
Look all the way around the car, starting on the right and finishing by looking into the left blind spot.

If you are unable to see behind you for any reason – for example, if luggage is obscuring your view through the rear window – you must get someone to guide you from outside the car. Never attempt to reverse if you are unable to see clearly on your own.

Manoeuvre

When you are sure it is safe to proceed, look backwards in the direction you are about to go and release the handbrake. Watch the position of the kerb relative to the reference point. If the kerb moves from that point, steer slightly in the same direction that the kerb appears to move. The faster or further it moves, the more you will have to steer. As soon as the kerb touches that point again, straighten your steering wheel. You may need to glance at the steering wheel to check that it is straight. Try to keep the kerb on the reference point all the time you are moving. You may glance occasionally into your left door mirror to double-check your position.

Every few seconds, glance forwards and into your right blind spot to see if anything is approaching. Try to set up a rhythmic pattern to your observations: try saying out loud 'Backwards, two, three, four, right, forwards, Backwards, two, three, four...'. Looking into your blind spot will be difficult if you have swivelled in your seat, but you must make the effort to turn and look properly – if a pedestrian crosses behind you, you may not see them until it is too late.

If anything does approach closer than about 20m while you are reversing, you must stop and let them pass. When you do stop, keep your foot on the footbrake so that anyone behind you can see your brake lights. If you just use your handbrake, they will only see a reversing light and may think that you are still moving; showing your brake lights as well lets them know that you have seen them and are stationary.

When you have reversed as far as you intended, brake to a stop, apply the handbrake and select neutral. Only then should you turn your body to face forwards again.

REVERSING INTO A SIDE ROAD ON THE LEFT

This manoeuvre begins and ends with a straight reverse – the new skill here is to steer accurately around the corner.

Approach

As you approach the side road, you must slow down and be ready to stop. Use the MSM/PSL routine as normal. If there is any traffic, you will need to signal your intentions, but take care with the timing of your signal. Use your brake lights to show that you are slowing down and only indicate left as you pass the side road: a vehicle emerging from the side road may think you are turning in if you signal too early, and may pull out in front of you.

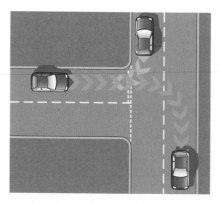

The correct route for reversing around a sharp corner on the left

As you reach the side road, look into it to check whether it is safe to reverse in. There may be an obstruction blocking your route, or children playing in the road. If necessary, drive on and find another place to reverse.

You must also assess the corner and decide whether it is a sharp turn or a sweeping one. The routine we are going to use will work with any type of corner, but you need to have an idea of how much steering you are likely to use before you reverse.

TIP
When you are driving forward normally, try to make note of how much you need to turn the steering wheel when turning left. This will help you to improve the accuracy of your assessment.

As a guide, you can make a quick guess at the number of kerb stones making up the corner: more than 8 would be a sweeping corner, less than 4 or 5 would be a very sharp turn.

Stop about one to two car lengths past the turning point. This is the first straight kerb stone after the corner. This allows any vehicle emerging from the side road to see past you and leaves them room to steer around you without too much difficulty. At this point, you should see the corner and some straight kerb in your left mirror.

TIP
Remember, *The Highway Code* states that you must not reverse further than is necessary (rule 203), so take care not to drive too far past the turning point.

As you will be not remain at a stop for long, you do not need to get as close to the kerb as you would normally park. As for the straight reverse, 20–30cm away is fine, but if the corner is very sharp you should stop further away – up to 50cm from the kerb.

Preparation
Apply the handbrake and select reverse before cancelling the indicator.

Observation
Make all round observations and check that it is safe to proceed. As you did for the straight reverse, establish the reference point where the kerb touches the bottom edge of the rear window.

Manoeuvre
When it is safe, reverse straight back slowly, using clutch control, until you see the kerb start to move across the back window.

TIP

As soon as it starts to move, check your right blind spot: the nose of the car will swing out into the road as you turn, so you need to be sure nothing is approaching.

Make most observations through the back windscreen when reversing

Glance in your left door mirror. This is now where you use your assessment of the sharpness of the corner. If you decided that it was a sweeping corner, you are going to wait until the kerb appears to touch the bottom edge of the mirror about halfway across, then steer half a turn towards the kerb, so your steering wheel is upside down. If you decided it was a very sharp corner, you will wait until the kerb is almost at the edge of the mirror and then steer one complete turn of the wheel towards the kerb. If you decided the corner was somewhere between sweeping and sharp, then wait until the kerb appears three-quarters of the way across the mirror, and then steer three-quarters of a turn towards the kerb.

If you are holding the steering wheel with your right hand only, you must briefly use your left hand as well. After making this first turn, grip the steering wheel at the '12 o'clock' position with your right hand and maintain this grip until you need to straighten up again.

As soon as you have made this first turn, look backwards, check your right blind spot and then have another glance in the door mirror.

The 'steering meter'

Use the left door mirror as a 'steering meter' to tell you how much you need to turn the steering wheel. The position of the kerb on the bottom edge of the mirror is your guide: if the kerb appears to be half-way across the mirror, turn the steering wheel so that it is half a turn towards the kerb (that is, upside down); if the kerb appears a quarter of the way across the mirror, that is between the side of the car and the half-way point, steer a quarter-turn towards the kerb. If the kerb appears close to the side of the car, you must straighten your steering wheel. If the kerb disappears from the mirror altogether, you must keep steering towards the kerb until it reappears in the mirror.

All of that has to be done in a glance. You can turn the steering wheel as you are looking backwards. Set up 'rhythmic observations', so that you are mainly looking through the rear window, glancing right and into the mirror. Remember to look into each road.

TIP

As you follow the corner, you might find that you get a better view into the road you have left from your mirrors. It is okay to use your mirrors as long as you also check your right blind spot each time you look around.

Follow the kerb around the corner, adjusting your steering each time you glance in the door mirror, until the kerb reappears in the rear window. Hold the steering wheel still until the kerb moves across the window back to the reference point you established at the start of the manoeuvre. As soon as the kerb reaches the reference point, steer away from the kerb to straighten your wheels.

Continue to reverse slowly in a straight line until the nose of your car is about three car lengths back from the junction. This allows any other vehicles space to safely negotiate the junction. Make sure you are still looking backwards as you stop and only face forwards again when you are stationary.

Apply the handbrake and select neutral. When it is safe, drive forwards and then signal to turn at the junction as directed.

Throughout the whole manoeuvre, you must make sure you are moving very slowly and looking all around the car. If anything approaches you, stop and wait for them to pass before continuing. The only exception to this rule is when the nose of your car has stopped swinging out and is retreating into the side road. During this phase of the reverse, if a vehicle approaches on the main road to your right, you should continue to reverse and make more room for the vehicle to pass. Listening for traffic may give you advance warning.

You may come across the situation where a vehicle approaches from behind and makes no attempt to pass you. If they have left enough room for you to continue and are obviously waiting, then carry on. Some drivers, however, may not spot your reversing light and will pull up right behind you. In this situation, you have no choice other than to abandon the reverse, pull forwards around the corner and start again when they have passed.

TIP

If you are turning left at the junction, make sure you are moving before you signal left – a left indicator on a stationary car means that it has just stopped or is staying still.

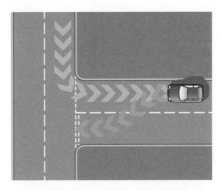

The arrows show the correct route for reversing round a corner on the right

REVERSING INTO A SIDE ROAD ON THE RIGHT

This manoeuvre uses the same techniques as the other reverses but involves being on the wrong side of the road, so extra care is required.

You won't have to perform this manoeuvre as part of your Driving Test, but if you are driving a van where vision through the rear is obscured, this is the preferred option.

Approach

As you approach the junction, use the MSM/PSL routine as if you were going to turn right, but do not indicate until you pass the side road. As you pass, check for obstructions, assess the corner and indicate right. Steer over to the right-hand side of the road, about 25cm from the kerb, and drive slowly forwards until you are about three car lengths past the junction. If anything approaches as you do this, you must stop and let them pass before continuing.

Preparation

Select reverse and find biting point.

Observation

Make careful all-round observations, beginning with your left blind spot. Position yourself in your seat so that you get a clear view of the kerb.

Manoeuvre

When it is safe, reverse straight back, looking at the kerb over your right shoulder. You can wind down your window and look out if you prefer (and you must use this method if you are driving a van), but remember you must also maintain continuous all-round observations.

When you reach the turning point, again come to a stop. Look all around the car and make sure it is safe to continue.

Looking over your right shoulder, steer around the corner using the same technique as for the left reverse.

TIP

Looking out of the window makes the steering a lot easier, as you will be able to see the rear wheel and the kerb.

When you are straight in the new road, continue to reverse slowly until you are about six car lengths back from the junction. Come to a stop and secure the vehicle.

Select first gear and make full all-round observations, finishing by checking your left blind spot. When it is safe, move off and steer briskly back to the normal side of the road. Immediately start the MSM/PSL routine for the junction.

As you are reversing on the wrong side of the road – something nobody will expect – you must be especially careful of other road users. Come to a complete stop if anything approaches from any direction, and allow them to pass. This manoeuvre should only ever be performed when there is no other alternative, and then only on a very quiet road.

PULLING UP ON THE OPPOSITE SIDE OF THE ROAD AND REVERSING

Find a suitable place on a straight, quiet road to practise.

Approach
As you approach the area where you are going to pull up slow down, use the MSM/PSL routine and remember to signal to the right. You will need to be especially vigilant for oncoming traffic. When there is a suitable gap in the traffic steer over to the right-hand side of the road, about 25cm from the kerb.

Preparation
Select reverse and find biting point.

Observation
Make careful all-round observations, beginning with your left blind spot. Position yourself in your seat so that you get a clear view of the kerb. Be particularly alert for cars pulling up behind you; if one does you will have to abandon the manoeuvre.

Manoeuvre
When you are sure it is safe to proceed, reverse straight back for about two car lengths, maintaining continuous all-round observations. When you have reversed as far as you intended, brake to a stop, apply the handbrake and select neutral.

To rejoin the traffic, select first, indicate left and make full all-round observations, paying close attention to any blind spots. When there is a suitable gap in the traffic, move off and steer briskly back to the normal side of the road.

Practice plan

First steps
Find a long, straight section of quiet road where you can practise the straight reverse. As you need to move your body so much, you may find clutch control to be more difficult than it was going forwards. Concentrate at first on maintaining a very slow speed.

When you are confident with the straight reverse, practise pulling up on the right-hand side of the road and then reversing.

Practise the left reverse on a quiet road where you are unlikely to be interrupted by other vehicles. Start with sweeping corners and make sure you are making effective observations. Try to get into a rhythm and act appropriately on any hazards you see.

Gaining confidence
When practising the straight reverse, deliberately start from an awkward position and practise getting back to a good position as quickly as you can. Try starting a long way from the kerb or at quite a sharp angle.

Practise reversing on a mixture of sweeping and sharp corners to the left.

Make sure you find a very quiet area to practise the right reverse.

Ready for the test
Make sure to practise all the reversing manoeuvres and ensure that you are confident with everything.

Avoid very busy areas when practising; *The Highway Code* specifically advises you to avoid such areas in rule 200.

Checklist

First steps	Gaining confidence	Ready for the test	
☐	☐	☐	Position for stopping
☐	☐	☐	Reference point on rear window
☐	☐	☐	Clutch control/speed
☐	☐	☐	Observations
☐	☐	☐	Acting appropriately on observations
☐	☐	☐	Accuracy of steering
☐	☐	☐	Straightening out correctly
☐	☐	☐	Finishing position

1

Before reversing there are three things to consider.

Fill in the missing words

1 Is it s___ ___ ___?

2 Is it c___ ___ ___ ___ ___ ___ ___ ___ ___?

3 Is it within the l___ ___?

2

Are the following statements about reversing true or false?

Tick the appropriate boxes

	True	False
1 Other road users should see what I am doing and wait for me.	☐	☐
2 I should wave pedestrians on, so that I can get on with the manoeuvre more quickly.	☐	☐
3 I should avoid being too hesitant.	☐	☐
4 I should avoid making other road users slow down or change course.	☐	☐

3

How should you hold the steering wheel when reversing left?

Which is correct? Answer ☐

A   B   C

4

When reversing, good observation is vital. Where should you look?

Tick the correct answer

1 At the kerb ☐

2 Ahead ☐

3 Where your car is going ☐

4 Out of the back window ☐

5

Are these statements about reversing round a corner true or false?

Tick the correct boxes

	True	False
1 If the corner is sharp, I need to be further away from the kerb.	☐	☐
2 The distance from the kerb makes no difference.	☐	☐
3 I should try to stay reasonably close to the kerb all the way round.	☐	☐

6

Before reversing I should check...

Tick the correct box

1 Behind me ☐

2 Ahead and to the rear ☐

3 My door mirrors ☐

4 All round ☐

7

When reversing into a side road on the left, which position is the correct one in which to start steering?

A, B, C or D? Answer ☐

8

Which way should you steer?

Answer _____

9

What will happen to the front of the car?

Answer _____

10

Are these statements about steering when reversing round a corner true or false?

Tick the appropriate boxes   **True** **False**

1 The more gradual, the corner the less I have to steer.   ☐ ☐

2 I need to steer the same for every corner.   ☐ ☐

3 The sharper the corner, the more I have to steer.   ☐ ☐

11

As I enter the new road, I should continue to keep a look-out for p__ __ __ __ __ __ __ __ __ __ __ and other r__ __ __ u__ __ __ __ __. I should s__ __ __ if necessary.

Complete the sentences

12

True or false? When reversing from a major road into a side road on the right, I have to move to the wrong side of the road.

Tick the correct box **True** ☐ **False** ☐

13

Which of the following correctly describes your sitting position for reversing to the right?

1 I will need to sit so that I can see over my right shoulder.

2 I will need to sit so that I can see over my right shoulder, ahead and to the left.

3 My position is the same as when reversing to the left.

Which statement is correct? 1, 2 or 3

Answer ☐

14

Reversing to the right is more dangerous than reversing to the left because...

1 I cannot see as well

2 I am on the wrong side of the road

3 I might get in the way of vehicles emerging from the side road

Which statement is correct – 1, 2 or 3?

Answer ☐

15

How far down the side road would you reverse before moving over to the left-hand side?

Which diagram is correct? A or B?

Answer ☐

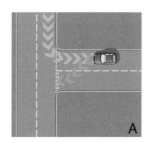

A

B

PARKING

There are two parking exercises you need to be able to carry out: parallel parking (parking parallel and close to the kerb between two parked cars) and bay parking (parking in a marked bay either on your left or your right). During your Driving Test you may be asked to perform one of these parking exercises.

How to do it

PARALLEL PARKING

The parallel park requires you to stop alongside another vehicle and then reverse into the space behind that vehicle, so that you park reasonably close and parallel to the kerb. Use the POM routine to guide you through the manoeuvre.

Approach

Approach the parked vehicle slowly, using your brake lights to show following traffic that you are slowing down. As you are level with the space, indicate left and look into the space to check that there are no obstructions. Stop just a little further forward than the parked car and about 75cm to 1m away. You should be able to see the headlights (or rear lights) of the parked car in your passenger's window. Apply the handbrake.

At this point, you may be blocking the whole road, so try to complete the next two steps as efficiently as possible.

Preparation

Select reverse and find biting point.

Observation

Make all-round observations and check that it is safe before continuing. If any vehicle approaches, wait and let them pass if they can, or wait until they are stationary.

LEGAL REQUIREMENTS
The Highway Code deals with waiting and parking in rules 238–252.

Manoeuvre

When it is safe, look through the rear window and reverse slowly, using clutch control to keep the car slow. As soon as you start moving, check the right blind spot: as you turn into the space the nose of your car will swing out further into the road. Looking backwards again, check that your rear seat is level with the back end of the parked car and then turn into the space by steering one turn towards the kerb.

Have another check in the right blind spot and then look backwards again. Alternate your observations between the rear window and the left door mirror. In the door mirror, you will see the kerb stones angling towards the side of the car. At the instant that the kerb disappears from that mirror, turn two complete turns away from the kerb.

TIP
Don't rush the steering, but the steering wheel should go round at about the same speed that your road wheels are turning.

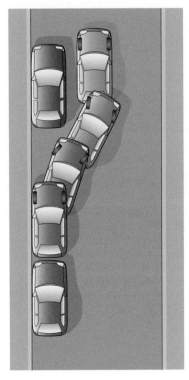

Reversing into a parking space requires a minimum gap of one-and-a-half car lengths

Alternate your observations between the rear window and the front corner of your car. Make sure that you don't let the corner of your car get too close to the parked car. As the nose of your car comes in you may find that you speed up slightly. This is because the front wheels are running down the camber of the road towards the kerb, so be prepared to brake gently.

Wait until you are straight. Look in your rear window to see the kerb moving across to your reference point (as in the left reverse). If there is another vehicle behind you, you might not be able to see the kerb. In this case you can keep glancing in the left door mirror. When you can see the kerb all the way down the side of your car and as far back as possible, you are straight.

As soon as you are straight, straighten your wheels by steering briskly one turn back towards the kerb. Apply the handbrake and select neutral. You are parked.

TIP
After every turn, your steering wheel should look straight, as it does when you are driving in a straight line.

Making corrections
With a little practice, you will find that the routine above works every time, provided you are consistent. If, however, you find that you regularly end up too far from the kerb, there are a number of possible reasons:
• You are steering right too quickly – make sure that you turn the steering wheel at the same speed that the road wheels are turning.
• You are moving too slowly – use clutch control to keep the car moving. Aim for about the same speed that you use when reversing around a corner. You don't want to go too slowly as you would block the road for longer than is necessary.

- Your left door mirror may be incorrectly positioned – make sure that you have adjusted it correctly as part of the cockpit drill.

If you are too far from the kerb, you will see the kerb in the left mirror well before you are straight. As soon as you see this, check your blind spot, steer back towards the kerb until it disappears again, then steer away again until you are straight. If you don't notice that you are too far away until you have stopped, pull forwards in a straight line until you are close to the parked car in front, then repeat the whole manoeuvre from this position (in reverse, blind spot, steer left one turn, kerb disappears, right two turns, when straight, straighten out and stop).

> **TIP**
> In reality, you may need to use full lock on every turn to get into tight spaces.

You may find that you touch the kerb before you manage to get straight. This could be because:
- You are steering right too slowly – make sure that you turn the steering wheel at the same speed that the road wheels are turning.
- You are moving too fast – use clutch control to keep the car moving slowly. Aim for about the same speed that you use when reversing around a corner. You don't want to go too slowly as you would block the road for longer than is necessary.

- Your left door mirror may be incorrectly positioned – make sure that you have adjusted it correctly as part of the cockpit drill.
- You are starting to turn right too late – make sure that you aren't distorting your view in the mirror by leaning over too far. Bob your head up or down so that you get the same view as when you originally positioned the mirror.

If you can see that you are too close to the kerb and will hit it if you continue, come to a stop. (On your test, tell the examiner that you need to pull forwards slightly to correct your position.) Make all-round observations and pull forwards slightly, steering as much to the left as you can, until you can see the kerb in the left door mirror again. Make all-round observations again and resume the manoeuvre (in reverse, blind spot, steer left one turn, kerb disappears, right two turns, when straight, straighten out and stop).

Summary
- Stop alongside and slightly forward.
- All-round observations.
- Reverse and blind spot.
- Back seat level with end of car.
- Steer one turn left into space.
- Kerb disappears from left door mirror.
- Steer two turns right, away from kerb.
- When straight, straighten wheels and stop.

BAY PARKING: REVERSING INTO A PARKING BAY ON THE RIGHT

Approach

As you approach the bay you intend to enter, slow down and maintain your normal road position on the left.

> **TIP**
>
> Don't get too close to any parked cars on the left, as you will need room for the nose of your car to swing out as you turn into the bay.

If there are other vehicles around, stop opposite the bay and indicate right in order to stake your claim. We shall label this bay 'bay one'.

When it is safe, drive slowly forward past bays one, two and three until the dividing line between bays three and four is level with your shoulder. Keep in your normal position, 1m from the left kerb. Stop and apply the handbrake.

Preparation

Select reverse gear, set a little gas and find biting point.

Observation

Make all-round observations and make sure it is safe.

Manoeuvre

When you are sure it is safe, look through the rear window and then release the handbrake. As soon as you start to move, steer towards the bay until you reach full lock. Make sure you time your steering so that the steering wheel turns at the same speed as the road wheels.

Check that the front-left corner of your car is not getting too close to the kerb or to parked cars on your left, and then look over your right shoulder to check that you are turning around the white line on the right of 'bay one'. If you think you are going to run over the line, steer away about half a turn until you are sure you are going to miss it, then reapply full right lock.

Glance to the left again, checking for any approaching vehicles or pedestrians.

When the white line on your right disappears from view, look into the left door mirror and wait until you start to see the white line on your left. As soon as it is visible, straighten your steering and then look to see if you are straight within the bay.

> **TIP**
>
> As you reverse in, compare your position with that of other parked cars or the white lines in front or behind you. If you are pointing left, steer left to straighten. If you are pointing right, steer right.

Look over your left or right shoulder to see how far back you can go. If there is a line at the front of the bays, let it move along the bottom sill of your door window until it is just below the door mirror.

Come to a stop, apply the handbrake and select neutral. You are parked.

TIP

If you feel you are not getting into the bay correctly, stop, pull forwards and straighten out in front of the bay. You can then straight reverse into the bay.

Summary

- Stop level with chosen bay.
- Check it is safe.
- Move forward to line between bays three and four.
- Reverse with full right lock.
- Check nose, then white line on right.
- Anything approaching?
- When white line disappears...
- White line in left door mirror.
- Straighten wheels.
- If not straight, steer the way you are pointing.
- Stop when front of bay appears just under right door mirror.

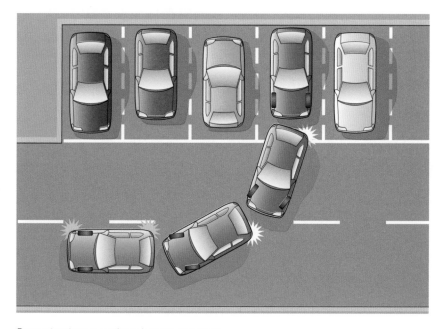

Reversing into a parking bay on the right

REVERSING INTO A PARKING BAY ON THE LEFT

You could reverse into a bay on your left using a mirror image of the previous method. This, however, would place you on the wrong side of the road for a substantial amount of time. The following routine is preferable in a busy car park.

Approach

Approach the empty bay as normal, and stop alongside it to check it is safe to reverse in. Use your indicator to stake your claim.

Preparation

Select first gear and find biting point.

Observations

Make all round observations finishing with a right blind spot check.

Manoeuvre

Move slowly forward, rechecking your right blind spot, until the far line of your chosen bay is level with your left shoulder. Steer briskly away from the bay to full right lock and hold the wheel still until you are at an angle of about 45°. This will be when you can see the white line you had just lined up with your shoulder, in the very bottom of your left door mirror. Stop, apply the handbrake, select reverse and find biting point. Make all-round observations again and, when it is safe, look through the rear window and release the handbrake. As soon as you start to move, steer into the bay, using full left lock. Turn the wheel briskly, but don't rush.

Check your right blind spot and the bay on your right to make sure that you are not too close. As soon as you can see the white line in your right door mirror, straighten your wheels and reverse straight back into the bay, stopping when you can see the front of the bay just underneath your door mirror. Apply the handbrake and select neutral. You have parked.

TIP

Whenever you are performing any manoeuvre and you feel it is going wrong, stop and pull forward far enough to be able to continue. Examiners will not usually allow you to start the whole manoeuvre again, but they will normally let you make corrections if necessary.

ENTERING A PARKING BAY FORWARDS

Parking in a marked bay forwards is probably harder than reversing in. The car is more manoeuvrable in reverse because the steering wheels are effectively at the back (as they are on shopping trolleys). It is also safer as you will have the best view when you leave.

Whichever side you intend to park, you will need to approach on the opposite side of the road, to about one car length away from the mouth of the bay. If you are parking in a bay on the left, approach on the right-hand side of the road – having made sure it is safe, of course. If you are parking in a bay on the right, approach on the left.

As you get close, make sure you look all around the car, especially into the blind spot in the direction you are going to turn. Steer straight until the nose of your car is level with the nearest white line of your chosen bay – the white line will appear under the door mirror on that side. If it is safe, turn briskly to full lock towards the bay. Make sure that you carefully watch both sides of your car to see that you don't get too close to another parked vehicle. As soon as you are straight, briskly straighten your wheels and inch forwards until you are fully inside the space. Stop, apply the handbrake and select neutral.

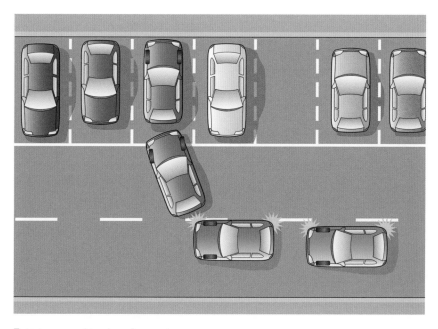

Entering a parking bay forwards

Practice plan

First steps
Practise the parallel park on a wide road, so that you won't have to worry about blocking the road. Try to find an area with low kerbs, so that you don't damage the tyres if it goes wrong.

Practising the bay park is increasingly difficult, as many supermarkets are starting to ban learner drivers from their land. Try to find a big car park with plenty of empty areas where you won't upset anyone. You may still need to ask permission to practise, and, if you get moved on by security, accept it with good grace and try to find somewhere else. If you use a council owned car park, be sure to purchase a ticket.

Gaining confidence
Practise the parallel park on normal roads. If you have two cars in your household, it would make sense to park one on the road so that you can practise on your own car.

Practise bay parking, both right and left, in spaces surrounded by other vehicles. You will probably find this easier than parking between empty spaces, as the parked cars give you a better idea of your own position.

Make sure that you also practise entering the bay nose first.

Ready for the test
Make sure that you practise parallel parking between vehicles of various sizes – anything from a Mini to a 50-ton truck. Practise parking into smaller gaps. As long as the gap is at least 1.5 times the length of your car you should be able to get in. Also remember to practise parallel parking on hills.

Find out whether your local Test Centre asks candidates to reverse bay park on their premises or not. If they do because of available space, check if there is any special method they expect you to use. If you wish to practise in the Test Centre, make sure you avoid the test appointment times. If the Test Centre is open in the evening it is better to practise then.

You should practise forward bay parking in any case, as this does not necessarily have to take place at the Test Centre.

Checklist

Parallel

First steps Gaining confidence Ready for the test

- [ ] [ ] [ ] Approach and start position
- [ ] [ ] [ ] Efficiency when stationary
- [ ] [ ] [ ] Observations
- [ ] [ ] [ ] Steering
- [ ] [ ] [ ] Speed
- [ ] [ ] [ ] Straightening out
- [ ] [ ] [ ] Accuracy
- [ ] [ ] [ ] Making corrections
- [ ] [ ] [ ] Securing the vehicle
- [ ] [ ] [ ] Hills
- [ ] [ ] [ ] Short spaces

Bay

First steps Gaining confidence Ready for the test

- [ ] [ ] [ ] Approach
- [ ] [ ] [ ] Observations
- [ ] [ ] [ ] Steering
- [ ] [ ] [ ] Speed
- [ ] [ ] [ ] Accuracy
- [ ] [ ] [ ] Between lines
- [ ] [ ] [ ] Between parked cars
- [ ] [ ] [ ] At Test Centre

1

When parking between two cars...

1 The car is more manoeuvrable when driving forwards

2 The car is more manoeuvrable when reversing

3 There is no difference between going into the space forwards or reversing into it

Which statement is correct? 1, 2 or 3?

Answer ☐

2

With practice you should be able to park in a gap...

1 Your own car length

2 1½ times your own car length

3 2 times your own car length

4 2½ times your own car length

Answer ☐

3

The diagram shows a car preparing to reverse into a parking space. Which position is the correct one in which to start steering left, A, B, C or D?

Answer ☐

4

Use the diagram to help you answer the following questions.

1 Which way would you steer?

Answer _____

2 At this point what would you try to line up with the offside (right-hand side) of your vehicle?

Answer _____

3 As you straighten up what do you have to be careful of?

Answer _____

4 What do you need to do to straighten up?

Answer _____

5 What would you need to do in order to position the vehicle parallel to the kerb?

Answer _____

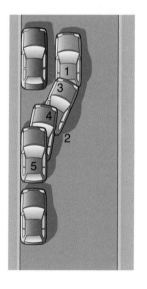

5

True or false? During my driving test...

Tick the correct boxes

	True	False
1 I will certainly be asked to perform the parallel park manoeuvre	☐	☐
2 I have to be able to park in a tight space between two cars	☐	☐
3 It may be that only one car is present during the parallel park	☐	☐

6

When carrying out the manoeuvre parking parallel and close to the kerb between two parked cars, where is it important to look?

Answer _____

7

Look at the diagram and answer the following question.

Which bay should you use and why?

Answer _____

_____

_____

8

Why, wherever possible, should you choose to reverse into a parking bay?

Answer _____

_____

_____

_____

9

As well as being very aware of how c__ __ __ __ I am to the parked cars on either side, I should also be alert for cars moving near me from all d__ __ __ __ __ __ __ __ __, as well as the possibility of p__ __ __ __ __ __ __ __ __ walking around my car.

Complete the sentence

_____

10

True or false? During my driving test...

Tick the correct boxes

	True	False
1 I will certainly be asked to perform a bay parking manoeuvre	☐	☐
2 I may be asked to forward park in a parking bay	☐	☐
3 My instructor will tell me what's expected of me	☐	☐

11

When might you choose to forward park in a parking bay?

Answer _____

_____

_____

_____

_____

12

When reversing out of a parking bay, I should be careful to o __ __ __ __ __ __ behind me before and during the manoeuvre, and be vigilant of p __ __ __ __ __ __ __ __ __ __ and other cars.

Complete the sentence

13

It is always best to park in a designated space. However, if you have to park on the road, list three places where you should *not* park.

1 _____

_____

_____

_____

_____

_____

2 _____

_____

_____

_____

_____

_____

3 _____

_____

_____

_____

_____

_____

TURNING IN THE ROAD

You need to be able to turn the car around in the road, using forward and reverse gears. You must make effective all-round observations and keep full control of the car's speed and steering. You will not be tested on your ability to turn in the road as part of your Driving Test, but it is a crucial skill for any driver to master.

How to do it

The 'turn in the road' is often wrongly referred to as the 'three-point turn'. Although it is likely that you will be able to turn the car around in three moves, this is not a requirement. The number of moves will depend on the width of the road and the length and turning circle of your car.

The manoeuvre consists of three (or five) move away and stop movements, and the POM (preparation–observation–manoeuvre) routine you use when moving away.

FIRST TURN
Preparation
Press down the clutch pedal and select first gear. Set a little gas and find the beginning of biting point. You will use clutch control to keep the car moving slowly, so don't bring the clutch up too high.

Observation
Make all-round observations, finishing with the right blind spot. Do not start the manoeuvre if you can see that you cannot safely reach the opposite kerb before an approaching vehicle would reach you.

LEGAL REQUIREMENTS
The Highway Code has no specific rules for this manoeuvre, but deals with reversing in general in rules 200–203.

Manoeuvre
When it is safe to do so, release the handbrake. As you move slowly forward, steer right to full lock as briskly as you can. As you start to turn, you may be going up the camber of the road (see below). As you are also steering so much, you may need to raise the clutch pedal very slightly to get up to the crown of the road. As you cross the crown, you will start to roll down the camber and may pick up speed. Be prepared to use the footbrake to control the speed of the car.

Roads generally slope down slightly at each side for drainage – this is the camber

Continue to hold full right lock until you see the kerb appear in your right side window just underneath the door mirror. At this point, the nose of the car is about 30cm from the kerb. As soon as it appears, steer briskly to the left as much as you can and, at the same time, gently brake to a stop. Apply the handbrake and select neutral.

TIP
Make sure you don't 'dry steer' – that is, turn the steering wheel when the car is stationary.

TIP
The exact position of the kerb as seen in the window will vary from car to car. If you are not sure where it should be in your car, reverse very slowly and ask your supervising driver to tell you when they think the rear of the car is about 30cm from the kerb. Stop there and see where the kerb appears, either in that window, your window or at the door pillar itself.

SECOND TURN
Preparation
Depress the clutch and select reverse. Set a little gas and find biting point.

Observation
Make all-round observations and finish by looking through the rear window.

Manoeuvre
When it is safe, release the handbrake. As the car moves slowly backwards, steer briskly to full left lock. As in the previous turn, you will be crossing the crown of the road, so be prepared to raise the clutch or brake to control the speed of the car. As soon as the car is straight across the road, at right angles to the kerb, look over your right shoulder. You are looking for the kerb to move into the nearest corner of the rear seat passenger's window, by the door pillar.

At this point, turn briskly to the right and gently brake to a stop. Apply the handbrake and select neutral.

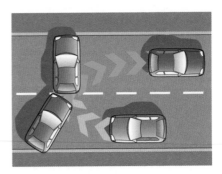

Turning in the road in three moves

THIRD TURN
Preparation
Depress the clutch and select first gear. Set a little gas and find the beginning of biting point. You will almost certainly be going up the camber of the road now, so be prepared to raise the clutch pedal slightly as you move off.

Observation
Make all-round observations starting behind you, as you are at an angle and close to the kerb, finishing with the right blind spot.

Manoeuvre
When it is safe, release the handbrake and steer right to return to the normal side of the road. When practising you should then pull over and park on the left.

TIP
Try to visualise the manoeuvre as a bird's-eye-view and look towards whichever wheel is nearest the kerb.

TIP
It is very unlikely that you will ever be asked to turn the car in the road where it would not be possible in five turns, but it is possible in real life. If you ever have to do this, continue to repeat the second and third turns, shuffling across the road until you have room to drive away.

FIVE TURNS
If the road is too narrow to complete the manoeuvre in three moves, repeat the second and third turns again.

In this case, the second turn that you make is unlikely to take you to a right angle to the kerb, so keep looking over your left shoulder to see the kerb.

The kerb will appear in the rear left passenger window, which is usually hidden by the front seat passenger. If this is the case, ask them to lean forwards so that you can see into that corner of the window. When you see the kerb there, turn right and stop as before.

On the third turn, you may get close to making it round, but if you didn't get to a right angle on the second turn, it is unlikely that you will make it, so don't take the risk. In this case, look for the kerb appearing underneath your left door mirror, and steer left, braking gently to a stop as in turn one.

Repeat the reverse leg (fourth turn), turning left as in the second turn, and then repeat the third turn (now the fifth) forward to complete.

GIVING WAY

When carrying out the 'turn in the road' manoeuvre, you will be blocking the road and must therefore give way to any other traffic.

If any vehicle approaches as you manoeuvre, finish the turn you are making and stop as normal. Prepare for the next turn, but give any waiting vehicles the opportunity to pass. If they choose to wait for you, continue the manoeuvre without rushing. Most other drivers will be quite happy to wait for you without getting impatient – they learned to drive themselves and will have done what you are doing. If the road is wide enough, they may choose to pass. You must remain stationary until you are certain that other vehicles are allowing you to continue.

TIP
The key to carrying out this manoeuvre successfully is to make sure that you move very slowly but steer briskly. Good clutch control is essential, as is good observation – always look in the direction you are moving.

Practice plan

First steps
Practise on a fairly wide but quiet road, where you will certainly be able to manage the manoeuvre in three moves.

Gaining confidence
Practise on narrower roads, where you will have to make five turns.

Ready for the test
This won't be on your test, but practise it anyway. Practise on a mixture of wide and narrow roads, including those with very steep cambers, on hills and on poorly surfaced roads.

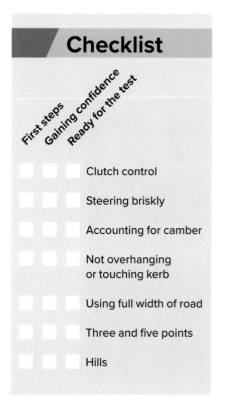

Checklist

First steps
Gaining confidence
Ready for the test

Clutch control

Steering briskly

Accounting for camber

Not overhanging or touching kerb

Using full width of road

Three and five points

Hills

1

Look at the diagrams and decide which is safer.

A Reversing into a side road

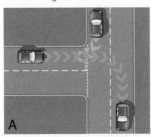

A

B Turning round in the road

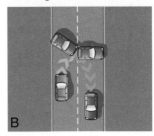

B

Answer ☐

2

The secret of turning in the road is to move the vehicle s__ __ __ __ __ and steer b__ __ __ __ __ __ __.

Complete the sentence

3

I must be able to complete the manoeuvre in three moves: 1 forward, 2 reverse, 3 forward. True or false?

Tick the correct box **True** ☐ **False** ☐

4

Before manoeuvring what should you take into consideration?

Tick the correct boxes

1 The size of your engine ☐

2 The width of the road ☐

3 The road camber ☐

4 The steering circle of your vehicle ☐

5 Parking restrictions ☐

5

Before moving forward, it is important to check a__ __ r__ __ __ __ for other road users.

Complete the sentence

6

Turning in the road requires proper use of the steering wheel.

Answer the following questions...

1 When going forwards, which way should you steer?

Answer _____

2 Before you reach the kerb ahead, what should you do?

Answer _____

3 When reversing, which way should you steer?

Answer _____

4 Before you reach the kerb behind you, what should you do?

Answer _____

5 As you move forward again, which way should you steer to straighten up?

Answer _____

7

Reversing is a potentially dangerous manoeuvre. Good observation is essential.

Answer the following questions

1 If you are steering left when reversing, which shoulder should you look over?

Answer _____

2 As you begin to steer to the right, where should you look?

Answer _____

KEEPING SPACE

You must always make sure that you have sufficient space around your vehicle. You must maintain a safe gap between yourself and the vehicle in front; space to the sides of your vehicle so that you do not get too close to other road users; and you should try to ensure an adequate distance behind you.

How to do it

WHEN YOU ARE MOVING
Ahead

The first rule concerns the space in front of your car. The 'Two-second Rule' tells you that you should maintain a gap of at least two seconds of travelling time between you and the vehicle in front.

To check this, find a fixed point in the road ahead, such as an arrow on the road, a road sign or a street lamp. As the vehicle in front passes that point start saying aloud 'Only a fool breaks the Two-second Rule.' You must be able to say this before you reach that same point. If you can't complete the phrase, slow down slightly and let the gap increase before trying again.

> **TIP**
> If you are good at judging distances, this works out at around 1m for every 1mph of speed.

On wet roads you must at least double this gap, as it will take longer for you to stop in an emergency. In icy conditions stopping distances increase ten times.

> **LEGAL REQUIREMENTS**
> *The Highway Code* refers to the spaces around a vehicle in rules 126, 151, 155, 192, 227, 230, 235, 239 and 260.

We will look at the use of speed in detail in the next section, but for now you must be familiar with and use the golden rule for speed: 'always drive at such a speed that you can comfortably stop in the distance ahead you can see to be safe.' For safety, never get closer than the overall stopping distance for the speed you are going.

At night you will need to drive more slowly, as the 'distance ahead you can see to be safe' is limited to the range of your headlights.

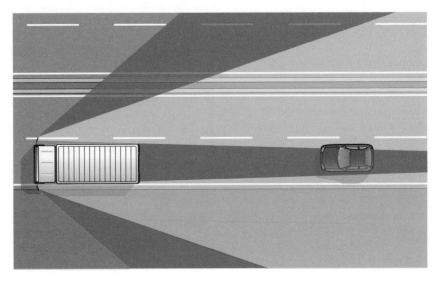

Remember that if you can't see a lorry's mirrors, the driver can't see you – the lorry's blind spots are in red

Behind

If a vehicle is driving too closely behind you, you need to increase the gap in front of you. This is to allow yourself time to give more warning if you are going to slow down. If the car in front of you had to stop suddenly, keeping the two-second gap would give you time to react safely and avoid running into it – but the car following too closely behind you would not have this time and would run into you.

If you increase the gap in front of you to include the gap for the following car as well, then you would have time to just show your brake lights for two seconds before you start to brake more firmly. This should give the other driver time to slow down before you do.

TIP

Persistent tail-gaters pose extreme danger to you.
When safe, you should indicate left, slow down and let them pass – you are much safer with them in front of you where you can see them more easily.

Sides

The general rule for positioning your car is that you should always be 1m from the side of the road or from any obstruction you need to pass. This metre gap is a safety margin in case a pedestrian steps off the pavement, or a car noses out over the Give Way line at a junction. If you are forced to get closer than 1m from the kerb, then you must slow down.

- You must maintain this 1m gap when passing parked cars or other obstructions. The door of a parked car could open as you pass, or a pedestrian could step out from behind a builder's skip.
- You should also allow at least a 1m gap on the right-hand side of your car. Never get closer to oncoming traffic than is absolutely necessary – a pedestrian could step off the pavement in front of an oncoming vehicle and the driver could swerve into you.

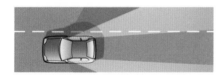

Be aware of other drivers' blind spots – shown here in red

- Always avoid driving alongside, or abreast of, another vehicle – leave space to improve your view, and allow room for manoeuvre.
- As a general rule, always try to drive with an imaginary bubble around your vehicle. If you have space all around, you have more options should you ever need to take emergency action, and more time to avoid ever having to take such action.
- Never drive in another driver's blind spot. This is particularly important on dual carriageways. Drop back so that you can see the driver's eyes in their side mirror – that way you know they can see you.

TIP

A similar rule applies when following large vehicles, such as lorries or coaches. If you can't see their mirrors, they can't see you.

Stationary

When stationary, use the 'Tyres and Tarmac' rule: always stop far enough behind the vehicle in front that you can see their tyres touching the road and 1m of tarmac.

This space leaves room for you to comfortably pull out and pass should the vehicle ahead break down. It also leaves you room to manoeuvre out of the way if an emergency vehicle needs to pass. You will also have room to react if the vehicle in front rolls back at a junction.

• Never stop so that you block access to a side road or business entrance. If oncoming traffic has to stop and wait for you to move it only adds to the congestion.

• If you have to stop alongside a parked car, allow room for the driver to open their door.

• When in queuing traffic, never stop on a pedestrian crossing – you may still be there when the lights change, which could force pedestrians to walk around you. This is doubly important for level crossings or marked tramways – the train or tram won't be able to stop for you.

• When you park, make sure you do not block access to driveways or side roads.

• Do not park opposite bus stops unless there is plenty of room for vehicles to pass between you and a bus waiting at the stop.

• Never park too close to a vehicle showing a disabled badge (see below) – the occupants may need room to put a wheelchair in the boot.

Practice plan

First steps
Practise using the 'Two-second Rule'. Using it consistently will ensure that you have more time to assess situations and avoid hurried reactions. You will find that your driving becomes smoother and more comfortable. Remember to multiply the time by two or ten in wet or icy weather.

Gaining confidence
In queuing traffic, practise the 'Tyres and Tarmac' rule. Make sure you use this rule whenever you pull up behind another vehicle.

Ready for the test
On dual carriageways or other multi-lane roads, practise avoiding driving in the blind spots or abreast of other vehicles. Be conscious of your position relative to other vehicles and make sure that they can see you.

Practise the 'Two-second Rule' on faster roads to see how much bigger the gap needs to be.

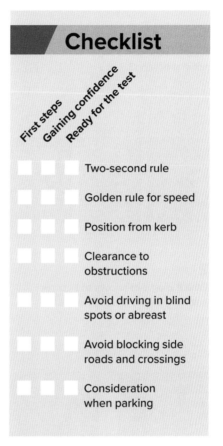

Checklist

First steps · Gaining confidence · Ready for the test

- Two-second rule
- Golden rule for speed
- Position from kerb
- Clearance to obstructions
- Avoid driving in blind spots or abreast
- Avoid blocking side roads and crossings
- Consideration when parking

1

Which is the correct position for normal driving?

Put letter A, B or C in the box

Answer ☐

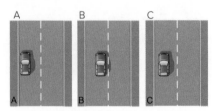

2

Which diagram shows the correct pathway when driving normally?

Put a letter A or B in the box

Answer ☐

3

Too many accidents are caused by drivers driving too close to the vehicle in front. A safe gap between you and the vehicle in front can be measured by noting a stationary object and counting in seconds the time that lapses between the vehicle in front passing that object and your own vehicle passing that object.

Complete the sentence

Only a fool b __ __ __ __ __ the t __ __
s __ __ __ __ __ rule.

4

When you observe traffic following too close behind you, would you

Tick the correct box

1 Speed up to create a bigger gap? ☐

2 Touch your brake lights to warn the following driver? ☐

3 Keep to a safe speed, and keep checking the behaviour and intentions of the following driver? ☐

5

It is safest to park off the road or in a car park whenever possible. If you have to park on the road, think...

Fill in the missing words

1 Is it s__ __ __ ?

2 Is it c__ __ __ __ __ __ __ __ __ __?

3 Is it l__ __ __ __ ?

6

In the diagram below, four of the cars are parked illegally or without consideration of others.

Put the numbers of these cars in the boxes

☐
☐
☐
☐

7

Are the following statements true or false?

Tick the appropriate boxes	True	False
1 In a narrow street, I should park with two wheels up on the pavement to leave more room for other traffic.	☐	☐
2 I am allowed to park in a 'Disabled' space if all other spaces are full.	☐	☐
3 I should not park on the zig-zag lines near a zebra crossing.	☐	☐
4 Red lines painted on the road mean 'No Stopping'.	☐	☐
5 I should never park on the opposite side of the road to my direction of travel.	☐	☐

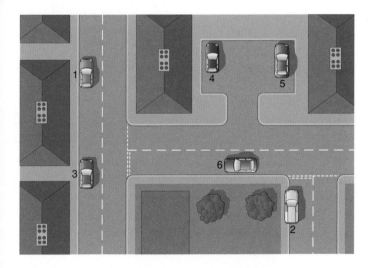

USE OF SPEED

You must always make sure that you are driving at an appropriate speed for the road and traffic conditions. When it is safe to do so, you should travel at the speed limit, making progress and not holding up other road users. You must be able to recognise situations where it would not be safe to travel at the speed limit and adjust your speed accordingly.

The dangers of speed: what you need to know

First, you need to appreciate the dangers of travelling too fast. Most people would agree that speeding is dangerous and yet the great majority of drivers speed on a regular basis. *The Highway Code* states categorically that you MUST obey speed limits and that those limits are exactly that – limits not targets.

If you are caught exceeding the speed limit the least you could expect to receive as punishment is a £60 fine and three penalty points on your licence. As a new or learner driver you will be allowed a maximum of five points within the first two years of driving (the probationary period). If you reach six points you will have your full licence revoked and you will have to start all over again. You will need to reapply for a provisional licence and take both your theory and practical tests again.

This, however, is unimportant compared to the potential danger you are creating by speeding. The speed limit on any particular road is set by road safety experts as the maximum speed it is safe to do. If you drive any faster than the speed limit, then you are less than safe and you pose a danger to other road users.

Consider the following scenario. You are driving along a 30mph road at 30mph when a child runs out in front of you.

LEGAL REQUIREMENTS
The Highway Code deals with speed limits and stopping distances in rules 124–126. Additional advice relating to speed can be found in rules 146 and 152–154. You must also be familiar with all the road signs and markings, especially those concerning speed limits and hazard warning signs.

You execute an emergency stop and manage to stop just before you hit the child. Before even touching the brakes you would have travelled 30 feet (10m), your thinking distance. It would take you a further 45 feet (15m) to brake to a stop, the braking distance, making a total of 75 feet (25m) to stop. Now consider what would happen if you were exceeding the speed limit by just 5mph. First of all, you would travel further before you react, in this case 35 feet (12m). You are now 5 feet (2m) closer to the child and still doing 35mph. It will now take you a further 61 feet (20m) to come to a stop, 21 feet (7m) past the child. Obviously you have just hit the child, but at what speed? The shocking answer is about 17mph. Most people, when asked this question, answer '5mph'.

Spotting potential hazards well in advance and dropping your speed accordingly is a vital skill for learners to develop – how many can you spot in the typical urban scene shown here?

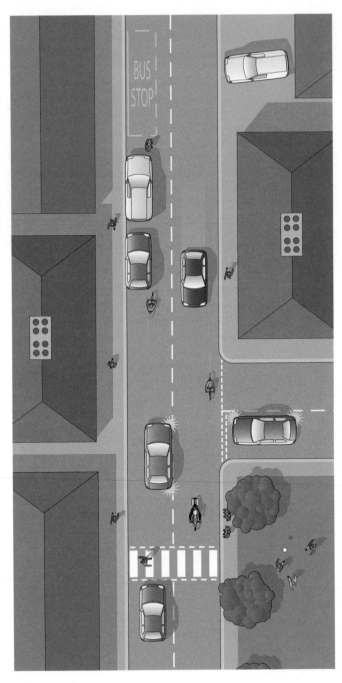

At 35mph you are twice as likely to kill someone as you are at 30mph.

The figures usually quoted for pedestrian fatalities are:

At 40mph: 9 out of 10 pedestrians are killed.

At 30mph: 5 out of 10 pedestrians survive.

At 20mph: 9 out of 10 pedestrians survive.

The important point here is that speeding kills. So how can you ensure that you are driving at a safe speed? There are two basic methods you can use to help you decide, depending on the speed limit of the road on which you are travelling.

HAZARD AWARENESS

Developing your hazard perception skills can greatly reduce your chances of having a collision – and therefore road deaths. When you are driving, you must be alert and aware of everything happening all around your vehicle. You have to spot potential problems and take avoiding action well before they develop into dangerous situations. This is the basis of both methods to ensure you are driving at a safe speed.

HOW TO DO IT

Driving in residential or built-up areas

On 30mph roads you must slow down for any hazard you see. If you take 5mph off the speed limit for each and every hazard, you will be going slowly enough to deal with the situation and prevent a collision.

By reducing your speed by 5mph for every additional hazard, you are creating time and space to deal with the various possible dangers.

Realistically, you would slow down to around no more than 15mph or even 10mph if you had to negotiate tight spaces between parked cars. At 15mph, an alert driver would be able to stop in less than one car length.

What to look out for

• In a residential area, there will be hidden driveways – a child could run out from behind the hedge, or a car reverse out of the drive, and pet cats or dogs are more likely to be crossing the road.

• In a busy town centre, pedestrians could step off the kerb to avoid obstructions, or cross the road unexpectedly. Can you watch every single pedestrian?

• Schoolchildren are unpredictable and can move very fast. You may have seen kids playfully pushing their friends into the road and catching them at the last moment ('Saved your life!'). What happens if they miss the catch?

- The door of a parked car on your side of the road could swing open as you pass, or the driver might pull away without checking their blind spot. The car could also hide a child stepping out behind it.
- Parked cars on the other side of the road can also pose a hazard. If there are parked cars on both sides, you are likely to be concentrating so much on your steering that you could easily miss seeing the child moving out into the road on their skateboard.
- At night it is much more difficult to see pedestrians or cyclists – even those who follow the advice in *The Highway Code* and wear brightly coloured reflective or fluorescent clothing.
- Bad weather can make it much harder to see: driving rain may not be adequately cleared by the windscreen wipers; mist and fog limit the distance you can see ahead; snow can be very disorientating; strong wind can affect your steering, and even bright sunshine can temporarily blind you and make it impossible to see into the shadows. Consider also that pedestrians are more likely to run with their heads down, or have their visibility reduced by hoods, hats, umbrellas, wet spectacles or eyes screwed up against the light.

These are just a few examples of the sorts of hazards you need to be wary of in built-up areas. You will be able to add to this list with many more from your own experience. Each and every hazard is a potential collision – only by slowing down 'in case' it develops will you be sure you are driving safely.

You must always expect the worst to happen when you are driving. Keep thinking 'What if...?' That way, you will be prepared for anything that does happen.

Adapting this for faster roads
On roads with a speed limit higher than 30mph, we can modify the above system slightly.

Warning signs
This first method is based around paying close attention to warning signs. Local authorities try to make sure that any hazard is well signed. Warning signs to tell motorists of approaching hazards are often grouped to encourage drivers to slow down further. Speed limits may be reduced where there are clusters of hazards.

As a general rule (though this cannot always be assumed), on main roads it would be safe to drive at the speed limit unless road signs or markings instruct you otherwise. To assess the appropriate speed for a major road, take 10mph off the speed limit for every different type of sign you see and for any additional hazards you can see that are not accounted for by the road signs or markings.

At the correct, slower speed the car stays level and travels more safely and comfortably (left); taking a bend too fast will cause the car to become unbalanced, lessening tyre grip on the road (right).

Take a look at the 60mph road in the picture on the right. You can see a warning triangle sign telling you that there is a bend to the right ahead. Slow down by 10mph to 50mph. On the bend itself, you can see the black and white 'sharp deviation of route' arrows or chevrons. Slow down by another 10mph. The signs and markings are telling you that you need to slow down to at most 40mph to take this corner safely.

Remember, any triangular sign gives a warning of a hazard, and every hazard is a place where you may have to slow down or steer. By slowing down when you first see the warning triangle, you are already prepared for the hazard should it materialise.

In addition, the positioning of the signs is often well planned, so that if you come off the gas as soon as you see the first sign (having checked your mirrors first, of course), then you will only need to brake very gently in order to slow to the appropriate speed.

Remember the golden rule: you should always be driving at such a speed that you can stop comfortably in the distance you can see ahead to be safe.

Method for cornering
The second method is about cornering at the correct speed and has two parts: balancing the weight of the car, and reading the road.

Gripping the road

You will know from experience that as you steer around a right-hand bend, your body and your centre of gravity are pushed over to the left, and vice versa. In the same way, when you accelerate your weight is pushed back into your seat, and forwards when you brake.

Let's assume that each tyre has 25 units of grip available, so there is a total of 100 units of grip for the whole car. To turn a corner, the tyres have to use these units of grip to change the direction of the car, and the faster you are going or the tighter the bend, the more grip you will need to turn the car. Let's say we require 60 units of grip to get around the bend in this particular example – that is, 15 units for each tyre.

As you turn right, the weight of the car is pushed to the left-hand side. The tyres on the left will now have to use more units of grip than the tyres on the right – say, the left tyres use 20 units and the right tyres use 10. Your left tyres now only have 5 units of grip remaining. If you have to slow down as you take the corner because, for example, a tractor has just turned out of a field in front of you, you can only brake using the remaining 5 units of grip. If you brake harder than this, you will run out of grip and skid. Worse still, as soon as you start to brake, the weight of the car is thrown forwards, so your front left tyre will need more grip than the rear one.

That is the tyre which will run out of grip first – one of the tyres that is steering you around the corner. As soon as it runs out of grip the car will no longer be able to turn and will go in a straight line, towards oncoming traffic.

There are many factors which can reduce the amount of grip your tyres have:
- the quality of the road surface
- the temperature of the tyres
- the condition of the tread on your tyres
- if the road is wet
- if your tyres are under- or over-inflated.

To get around the corner without skidding or sliding, you must make sure that the grip required of each tyre never exceeds the amount it can provide.

In order to keep the weight of the car more evenly distributed over all four tyres, you must try to keep the centre of gravity as close to the centre of the car as possible. If you slow down to a safe speed and start to accelerate very gently before you start to turn, the weight of the car will be pulled back towards the centre, putting less demand on the front tyres. This not only gives a much more comfortable ride for you and your passengers, but is also much safer, as the weight of the car is more evenly distributed over the four tyres, making them much less likely to run out of grip.

Judging the bend

The second part to this system is to make sure that you read the road accurately. This system is actually part of advanced driver training, but is equally valuable for the learner driver.

It can be very difficult to judge how tight a corner or bend is, so you need to learn to assess the severity of the bend and the correct speed to use.

Let us just recap the golden rule for speed: **You should always be driving at such a speed that you can stop comfortably in the distance you can see ahead to be safe.**

Imagine that you are on a national speed limit road (60mph), approaching a right-hand bend after a long straight. At the moment, there is no reason for you to be travelling at less than 60mph, and you are in fifth gear. You can see a warning triangle ahead, telling you that the road bends sharply to the right. This sign

will be around 100m from the start of the bend – slightly further than the overall stopping distance at 70mph (96m). But, because the road bends to the right, as you pass the sign you will not be able to see as far ahead as you would on a straight road.

You should always look to see how far ahead the vanishing point is – that is, the point at which the two sides of the road appear to meet. When the vanishing point is 50m ahead, you should be travelling no faster than 50mph because the overall stopping distance at 50mph is 53m. The table above shows the overall stopping distances at various speeds.

From the table below, you can see that if the vanishing point is 40m ahead, then the maximum safe speed is 40mph because at that speed you can stop in 36m. If you use this system you can be sure that you are never going too fast for the bend.

OVERALL STOPPING DISTANCE	SPEED
12m	20mph
23m	30mph
36m	40mph
53m	50mph
73m	60mph

So, the closer you get to the vanishing point, the slower you must go.

When you are at the correct speed for that particular corner, the vanishing point will appear to stay the same distance away.

As you steer around the bend, the vanishing point will start to get further away as the road starts to straighten out. At this point you can start to accelerate gently out of the bend.

We could summarise this system by saying:

- If the vanishing point is getting closer to you, slow down.
- If the vanishing point is keeping a constant distance, you are at the right speed.
- If the vanishing point is moving away from you, gently accelerate.

And the golden rule: Always drive at such a speed that you can stop comfortably in the distance ahead you can see to be safe.

TIP
It's better to learn stopping distances than to have to learn by your mistakes. Don't let your experience of near-misses teach you about safety margins the hard way.

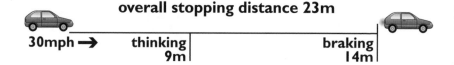

overall stopping distance 23m

30mph → thinking 9m   braking 14m

A stopping distance is made up of a thinking distance and a braking distance

Stopping Distances

20 mph

6 metres + 6 metres

= 12 metres (40 feet) or 3 car lengths

30 mph

9 metres + 14 metres

= 23 metres (75 feet) or 6 car lengths

40 mph

12 metres + 24 metres

= 36 metres (118 feet) or 9 car lengths

50 mph

15 metres + 38 metres

= 53 metres (175 feet) or 13 car lengths

60 mph

18 metres + 55 metres

= 73 metres (240 feet) or 18 car lengths

70 mph

21 metres + 75 metres

= 96 metres (315 feet) or 24 car lengths

Thinking Distance

Braking Distance

The average car length is 4 metres (13 feet)

Practice plan

First steps

Practise spotting hazards as you drive. At first just say 'hazard' out loud, then gradually become more specific, saying 'parked car' or 'child on bike'. Remember to include every road sign you see, and try to make sure you spot them as soon as possible.

Learn the overall stopping distances from *The Highway Code* and also make sure you know what the speed limits are on various types of roads.

Also practise judging distances in metres. Try estimating the distance from your parked car to a junction, a lamppost or another parked car. Pace it out and see how accurate you are.

Gaining confidence

Practise spotting hazards as you drive around built-up areas and, for each one, check your mirrors and slow down by 5mph to a minimum of around 15mph.

On faster roads, spot the road signs as soon as you can and reduce the maximum speed limit by 10mph for each different sign. Make sure that you always follow the golden rule for speed.

Find a national speed limit road that has a few good bends. Practise watching the vanishing point and adjust your speed accordingly.

Ready for the test

Get your supervising driver periodically to ask you what the speed limit is. You should always be right.

You should always be driving within the maximum speed limit, making progress when it is safe and reducing your speed when it is not safe. Make sure that you use the MSM/PSL routine for every hazard you see.

As you corner on faster roads, try saying out loud what the vanishing point appears to be doing, for example, 'The vanishing point is getting nearer, so I'm checking my mirrors and slowing down. Now it's staying still so I'm gently on the gas keeping a steady speed. Moving away, so gentle acceleration back to speed limit.'

Again, on faster roads, commentate on the road signs you see. For example, 'Crossroads warning sign, so maximum speed is 50. Past that so back to 60. Now, Double Bend sign so maximum 50. SLOW on road, maximum 40 –' and so on.

Try 'commentary driving' in built-up areas. This requires you to say out loud what hazards you see, what they could cause you to do and the actual action you take. Because you speak about five times more slowly than you can think, this forces you to look further ahead and act on what you see sooner.

Don't worry if it sounds like gibberish at first – with practice you will get more fluent and should see a dramatic improvement in your driving. It's well worth your time asking your driving instructor for a demonstration. Commentary driving has such a dramatic effect on developing driver awareness and planning, it is worth devoting an hour or so to it as you get closer to taking your practical test.

Checklist

First steps   Gaining confidence   Ready for the test

Highway Code

- Stopping distances
- Speed limits
- Hazard perception
- Judging distances
- Built-up areas: -5mph for each hazard
- Faster roads: -10mph for each hazard

Cornering

- Slow down before
- Gently accelerate through
- Accelerate out
- Balance of car
- Following vanishing point
- Golden rule
- Commentary driving

1

Could these factors affect thinking distance?

Tick the appropriate boxes   **YES**   **NO**

1 The condition of your tyres ☐ ☐

2 Feeling tired or unwell ☐ ☐

3 Speed of reaction ☐ ☐

4 Going downhill ☐ ☐

2

Most drivers' reaction time is well over...

Tick the appropriate box

½ second ☐

1 second ☐

5 seconds ☐

3

Stopping distance depends partly on the speed at which the car is travelling.

Complete the sentences

1 At 30mph your overall stopping distance will be __ __ metres or __ __ feet.

2 At 50mph your thinking distance will be __ __ metres or __ __ feet.

3 At 70mph your overall stopping distance will be __ __ metres or __ __ __feet.

4

Stopping distance also varies according to road conditions.

Complete the sentences

In wet weather your vehicle will take l __ __ __ __ __ to stop. You should therefore allow m __ __ __ time.

5

As a rule you should be travelling at the correct s__ __ __ __, using the correct g__ __ __, and be in the correct p__ __ __ __ __ __ __.

6

Should you brake...

Tick the appropriate box

1 Before you enter the bend? ☐

2 As you enter the bend? ☐

3 While negotiating the bend? ☐

7

Which way does force push a car on a bend?

A Inwards or **B** Outwards

Answer ☐

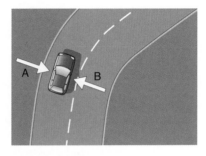

8

What happens to the weight of the car when you use the brakes?

A It is thrown forwards

B It remains even

C It is thrown back

Answer ☐

9

When you approach a bend, what position should you be in?

Complete the sentences

A On a right-hand bend I should keep
to the _____
_____

B On a left-hand bend I should keep
to the _____
_____

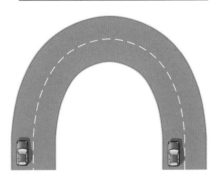

ADVERSE CONDITIONS

You must be able to drive safely in adverse weather conditions. You should know how to modify your driving to maximise safety, and how to operate any controls required to improve visibility. Many of the rules for driving in adverse weather also apply to driving at night.

How to do it

Adverse driving conditions are any conditions where your driving may be affected by the weather or road conditions. The two major aspects covered in this section are: visibility and control. Most poor weather conditions will affect both of these, but even on the sunniest of days you may need to modify your driving to account for the conditions.

Visibility

Poor weather can greatly reduce visibility – not only how far ahead you can see, but also how easy it is for others to see you. Fog, mist and rain will all reduce your visibility. If you are not able to see further than 100m ahead, you must use your headlights. You may also use fog lights, but you must turn them off when visibility improves.

> **TIP**
> If you need to put your lights on, use headlights. There is no occasion when sidelights are suitable, other than for parking.

It can be difficult to judge when to put your lights on in daylight, so be guided by other drivers. If you can see that other drivers are using their headlights, then use yours – you don't want to be any less visible than they are. There will always be some vehicles with sidelights on, as all new cars are fitted

> **LEGAL REQUIREMENTS**
> Rules 226–237 of *The Highway Code* deal directly with driving in adverse weather conditions. Rules 110–115 deal with use of lights and horn, rule 132 gives information on coloured cat's eyes on the road, and rules 248–251 concern parking at night and in fog.

with daytime running lights (DRL), however, it is your headlights you need on. Consult your car's handbook to see if your car is fitted with automatic lights.

If the weather is making it difficult for you to see, make sure you use the windscreen wipers (you should have found out how to operate them in the first lesson) on an appropriate setting. If fitted, you may also need to use the rear window wiper so that you can see in your mirror. It is not just rain that may obscure your windscreen – any precipitation, including fog and mist, will also require the use of the wipers.

In cold weather your windows may mist up inside. Use the de-mist settings of your heaters and, if fitted, the heated windscreen to clear them.

If the outsides of your windows freeze, you must clear them before driving. Keep a can of de-icer in the car and in the house. In really cold weather, you may not be able to open the doors until the ice has thawed. Never use hot water to de-ice your windows – you might crack the glass or break the waterproof seals. If you must use water, make sure it is no hotter than you could comfortably hold your hand in, and remember that while you go to get a refill, the water could well freeze on the windscreen again.

Make sure that you use an appropriate anti-freeze in your washer bottle. It is an offence to drive without the means to clean your windscreen, and in cold weather, the salt thrown up from gritted roads will mean you need to clean your windscreen much more frequently. If the water in the washer bottle and pipes has frozen, add warm water to the bottle and start the engine. Allow the heat from the engine to thaw the lines before driving on. At the first opportunity, add more winter screenwash to prevent the washer bottle freezing again.

TIP

If you are struggling to see, you may find it useful to wind your front windows down at junctions: you may hear approaching traffic before you see it.

Control

The weather can also affect your control of the car. Wet or icy roads will greatly increase your stopping distances, so increase the separation distance in front of you (see Section 17). If the roads are icy or covered by snow, avoid driving unless your journey is essential, and then take the utmost care.

ICE OR SNOW

- If you must drive in these conditions, reduce your speed and increase the separation distance from the vehicle in front to at least ten seconds.
- If you drive on ice, you will hear little noise from your tyres, warning you that you have very little traction. Drive as smoothly as possible, making every change of speed or direction as gentle as you can.
- Brake only when you're moving in a straight line – never while turning.
- Try to use the highest gear you can for the speed you are going – using fourth gear at 20mph would be reasonable in these conditions. This gives less power at the road wheels and will help you to avoid losing traction.
- Watch out for ruts in the snow or ice, as these can be difficult to get out of and the road conditions may take over control of your steering.
- Watch out for gritting lorries or snowploughs, which can throw chunks of ice or grit all over your vehicle.
- Listen to the local weather forecast or news programmes for police advice about driving in such conditions.

RAIN

Avoid driving through puddles if at all possible. If the puddle is deeper than you thought, it can pull your steering towards the kerb. You will not know what is at the bottom of the puddle – it could be a deep pot-hole, or even hide broken glass. You must never splash pedestrians; this is an offence and the police will pursue it if reported. If you have to go through a puddle slow down, and if there are pedestrians around, slow down even more so that you don't splash them.

Standing water on faster roads can cause your car to aquaplane. This occurs when the tyre tread is unable to move the water quickly enough and the tyres lose contact with the road surface. Essentially, your car is then water-skiing. You will lose control completely until the car drops enough speed for the tyres to cope with the amount of water. If this happens to you, ease off the gas pedal and hold your steering wheel straight. Don't attempt to brake. Wait until you hear tyre noise on the road again and the steering feels responsive before slowing down to a safer speed. Avoid the dangers of aquaplaning by slowing down if you see standing water across the road.

FORDS AND FLOODS

If you have to drive through deep water – for example, a flood, or a ford – you should test your brakes immediately afterwards. To do this, at a slow speed of no more than 10mph, check your mirrors then brake gently and check that

you do slow down. If the brakes are affected by water, you may need to dry them by maintaining a slow speed, using a little gas, while at the same time braking very gently with your left foot for about 5 seconds. Test your brakes again and repeat the process if necessary.

TIP
This is the only situation in which you ever use your left foot on the brake pedal.

WIND

Windy weather is most likely to affect larger, high-sided vehicles such as lorries, but strong gusts can blow a car off course. Be careful when moving between open and sheltered areas, and when passing lorries. Look out for other road users who are likely to be blown around, particularly drivers of high-sided vehicles, motorcyclists, cyclists, and drivers towing caravans or trailers.

Watch out for debris blown by the wind such as fallen branches, roof tiles and plastic bags. Be especially careful in rural areas where even moderate winds can cause branches to fall from trees.

SUN

Believe it or not, the sun can cause adverse conditions, too. The temperature on a hot sunny day can be sufficient to melt the tarmac and the road surface can become soft and slippery. Roads constructed with loose chippings can melt enough for stones to be thrown up by the vehicle in front, so keep well back.

Low sun can be a problem at any time of year. If the sun is directly in your line of sight, it can effectively blind you. Reduce your speed and use your sun visor to shield your eyes if possible.

TIP
Wearing sunglasses will not help combat low sun, as the long shadows will just become even darker, hiding anything that may be in them.

You will also find that the effects of low sun are much worse if your windscreen is dirty. Use the windscreen washers to clean the outside, and stop to clean the inside of the screen if necessary. If you wear glasses, make sure that they are clean as well.

NIGHT DRIVING

At night, you must use your headlights so that you can see the road ahead and be seen by other road users. Make sure your lights are clean and in working order, checking them before you start any night-time journey. Headlights have two settings: 'dipped' and 'main beam'. Main beam will improve your view of the road ahead but will also dazzle any road users ahead of you. Make sure you use the dipped setting if there is any vehicle in front of you. If your car is fitted with auxiliary lights, sometimes called spotlights, they must be wired so that they operate in tandem with your main beam.

You must use headlights during the published 'lighting up time' and is a legal requirement. This time is defined as the period between half an hour after sunset and half an hour before sunrise. As soon as you see the streetlamps begin to come on, put your headlights on, although you shouldn't rely on this method. Don't be afraid to be the first car to have lights on and if your car is a dark colour, switch on sooner.

TIP
Find sunrise and sunset times next to the weather forecast in daily papers or online.

Speed

On unlit roads, your view is limited to the extent of your lights. When applying the golden rule for speed (Always drive at such a speed that you can comfortably stop in the distance you can see ahead to be safe), remember that you can only see as far as the range of your headlights. You must drive slowly enough to be able to stop in this distance.

> **TIP**
> Cat's eyes in the road surface are often visible further ahead than the range of your headlights. Different colours are used to show lane divisions, the sides of the road and slip roads.

It is much harder to see pedestrians, cyclists and animals at night. By slowing down, you will give yourself time to look more carefully.

Light coloured or fluorescent clothing is more easily seen than dark clothing, but only reflective materials show up well at night. Carry a reflective jacket and a torch in the boot in case you need to make repairs at the roadside or walk to a telephone.

It is much more difficult to judge speed and distance at night, so take great care at junctions and in meeting situations. Be especially careful of road users who are less visible.

Dazzling

As you set off on a journey at night, allow a minute or so for your eyes to get used to the darkness before you start to drive. You can use this time to check and clean your lights, mirrors and windscreen. Always make sure that your windscreen is thoroughly clean when driving at night: clean glass cuts down the dazzle of oncoming lights.

Avoid looking directly at oncoming traffic – even dipped headlights can dazzle. Instead, keep your eyes focused on the left-hand kerb at the limit of the range of your own lights.

> **TIP**
> Your main mirror may have an anti-dazzle switch that still allows the same field of vision but dims the whole view. Only use it if you are being dazzled by a vehicle behind you, and remember to turn it back to the normal setting when that vehicle is no longer dazzling you.

Make sure you don't dazzle other road users. Keep well back: your light beam should not touch the vehicle in front.

If you are dazzled by approaching lights, slow down and stop if necessary. Don't retaliate by turning your lights to main beam, but a very quick flash of your main beam should be enough to remind the other driver of your presence, and to dip their lights.

TIP
If you are transporting a heavy load, the weight in the back of your car may raise the angle of your headlights. To avoid dazzling drivers ahead, use the headlight adjuster, if fitted, to lower the angle of your lights.

Avoid keeping your foot on the brake pedal when you have stopped, for example in a queue of traffic: the brightness of your brake lights will dazzle the driver behind you.

Parking
On a 30mph (or less) road, you may park without lights, but you must be facing the same way as the traffic flow. If you have to park on a faster road, use sidelights or parking lights.

Whenever you park, even for a short time, turn off your headlights and use sidelights instead.

Noise
Remember the rule about using your horn: you must not sound your horn between the hours of 11.30pm and 7am except to avoid danger from a moving vehicle. Use flashed headlights instead.

Keep all noise to a minimum at night. Don't rev the engine or slam doors, and be extra careful when setting or disarming your car alarm.

Summary
In any adverse conditions, you should slow down and increase the separation distance between you and the vehicle in front. In severe conditions, avoid driving unless it is absolutely necessary.

Practice plan

As you have no control over the weather, you must simply take the opportunity to practise as it arises. Avoid driving in really bad weather until you are happy with every other aspect of driving.

If you get the chance to experience driving in poor weather conditions, remember to slow down, increase the gap in front and use your lights when necessary.

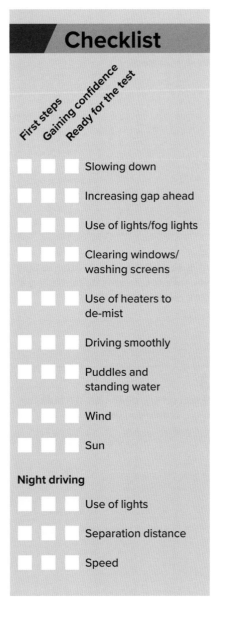

Checklist

First steps | Gaining confidence | Ready for the test

☐ ☐ ☐ Slowing down

☐ ☐ ☐ Increasing gap ahead

☐ ☐ ☐ Use of lights/fog lights

☐ ☐ ☐ Clearing windows/ washing screens

☐ ☐ ☐ Use of heaters to de-mist

☐ ☐ ☐ Driving smoothly

☐ ☐ ☐ Puddles and standing water

☐ ☐ ☐ Wind

☐ ☐ ☐ Sun

Night driving

☐ ☐ ☐ Use of lights

☐ ☐ ☐ Separation distance

☐ ☐ ☐ Speed

1

Which of these statements do you think is correct?

Tick the correct box

1 Street lighting and my car's headlights mean that I can see just as well as in the daylight. Therefore driving at night is just like driving in the daylight. ☐

2 At night I have to rely on my car's headlights and any additional lighting. Therefore I cannot see as far or drive as fast as in the daylight. ☐

2

At dusk and dawn what action should you take to compensate for driving a dark coloured car?

Answer _____

_____

_____

3

When driving after dark in a built-up area, should you use...

Tick the correct box

1 Dipped headlights? ☐

2 Side or dim-dipped lights? ☐

4

The diagram below illustrates two vehicles parked at night on a two-way road.

Which one is parked correctly?

Tick the correct box

A ☐   B ☐

5

Under what circumstances would you use dipped headlights during the day?

Answer _____

_____

and then complete the sentence

S__ __ and b__ s__ __ __.

6

When you are waiting at a junction after dark, your brake lights might d__ __ __ __ __ the driver behind. It is better to use your h__ __ __ __ __ __ __ __.

Complete the sentences

7

Which of the following causes greatest danger to drivers?

Tick the correct box

1 Snow ☐

2 Ice ☐

3 Heavy rain ☐

4 Not being able to see properly ☐

8

In wet weather conditions your tyres can lose their grip.

You should allow at least d__ __ __ __ __ the distance between you and the car in front that you allow on a dry road.

Fill in the missing word

9

In very wet conditions there is a danger of a build-up of water between your tyres and the road.

This is called a__ __ __ __ __ __ __ __ __ __.

Fill in the missing word

10

How can you prevent a build-up of water occurring?

S__ __ __   d__ __ __ .

11

How should you deal with floods?

Tick the correct box

1 Drive through as fast as possible to avoid stopping ☐

2 Drive through slowly in 1st gear, slipping the clutch to keep the engine speed high ☐

3 Drive through in the highest gear possible, slipping the clutch to keep the engine speed high ☐

12

When the tyres lose contact with the road, the steering will feel v__ __ __ l__ __ __ __.

Complete the sentence

13

After you have driven through a flood, should you check...

Tick the correct box

1 Your speedometer? ☐

2 Your brakes? ☐

3 Your oil? ☐

14

There are certain key precautions you should take when driving in fog.

Complete the following sentences

1 S__ __ __ d__ __ __ __.

2 Ensure you are able to s__ __ __ within the distance you can see to be clear.

3 Use your w__ __ __ __ __ __ __ __ __ __ w__ __ __ __ __.

4 Use your d__ __ __ __ __ __ __ and your h__ __ __ __ __ r__ __ __ w__ __ __ __ __ __ __ __ __.

15

Under what circumstances should you use your rear fog lights?

When visibility is less than _____ metres/feet.

Fill in the correct number

16

When you are following another vehicle in fog, should you...

Tick the correct box

1 Follow closely behind because it will help you see where you are going? ☐

2 Leave plenty of room between you and the vehicle in front? ☐

17

When you are following another vehicle in fog, should you use...

Tick the correct box

1 Main beam headlights? ☐

2 Dipped headlights? ☐

18

Extra precautions are needed when dealing with a junction in fog.

Complete the following sentences

1 Open your w__ __ __ __ __ __ and switch off your a__ __ __ __ s__ __ __ __ __. L__ __ __ __ __ for other vehicles.

2 Signal e__ __ __ __ __ .

3 Use your b__ __ __ __ __ __. The light will a__ __ __ __ following vehicles.

4 Use your h__ __ __ if you think it will w__ __ __ other road users.

19

When driving in snow or ice you should gently test your b__ __ __ __ __ __ from time to time.

Fill in the missing word

20

In order to slow down when driving on snow or ice you should...

Fill in the missing words

1 Use your brakes g__ __ __ __ __ .

2 Get into a l__ __ __ __ g__ __ __ earlier than normal.

3 Allow your speed to d__ __ __ and use b__ __ __ __ __ gently and early.

21

On snow or ice, braking distances can increase by...

Tick the correct box

1 10 times ☐

2 5 times ☐

3 20 times ☐

4 15 times ☐

22

When going downhill in snow, what would you do to help you slow down?

Answer _____

_____

_____

23

When cornering in snow or ice, what should you avoid doing?

Answer _____

_____

24

How can you reduce the risk of wheel spin?

Answer _____

_____

_____

25

Three important factors cause a skid.

Name them.

1 _____

_____

2 _____

_____

3 _____

_____

26

Some everyday driving actions, especially in poor weather, can increase the risk of skidding.

Fill in the missing words

1 S__ __ __ __ __ down.

2 S__ __ __ __ __ __ up.

3 T__ __ __ __ __ __ corners.

4 Driving u__ __ __ __ __ and d__ __ __ __ __ __ __.

VULNERABLE ROAD USERS

You must demonstrate that you are aware of the needs of more vulnerable road users, that you show them due consideration and drive with their safety in mind.

How to do it

The examiner will expect you to drive with the safety of others in mind at all times. You must be especially careful of pedestrians, cyclists, motorcyclists and horse riders. Be especially considerate towards learner drivers, emergency vehicles, public transport vehicles and lorries.

As an inexperienced driver, pedestrians and cyclists may be your biggest worry, as both of these groups can be very unpredictable, especially children.

- Wherever you are likely to meet pedestrians in shopping or residential areas, drive carefully and slowly. Take special care when passing parked vehicles – pedestrians could emerge suddenly or without looking. Particularly likely places are: at or near bus or tram stops and stations; ice cream or burger vans; near schools and playgrounds, and near roundabouts or large junctions.
- Look out for elderly people and children who may underestimate your speed and overestimate their ability to cross the road. Remember, elderly people are likely to move more slowly, taking more time to cross, while children move much more quickly and may appear out of nowhere.
- Be considerate of those pedestrians with disabilities such as blindness, deafness, walking difficulties, and people in wheelchairs. Give them plenty of room and time to cross the road and do not harass them by beeping the horn, revving the engine or edging forward.

LEGAL REQUIREMENTS
The Highway Code has a whole section on 'Road users requiring extra care', which links to rules 204–225. Also read 195 and H2–H3.

TIP
Watch out for the electric scooters used by some disabled people. They are very small and can be difficult to spot.

- Be very careful around schools, playgrounds and school buses. Pre-adolescent children have not yet developed the ability to judge speed accurately at all, and may think they have plenty of time to cross when, in reality, they don't. Some children don't understand the consequences of certain types of behaviour, and they may play dangerous tricks on their friends such as 'playing chicken'.

- While some cyclists, especially children, can behave as unpredictably as pedestrians, they are more of a potential hazard because of their higher speed.
- Younger cyclists may not be in full control of their bike. You must also bear in mind that they are much more susceptible to poor road surfaces, drain covers and other obstructions, the weather and the actions of other road users. They may be forced off course suddenly by obstacles in the road, and into your path. Give them plenty of room.
- Be careful of cyclists at night. They are much more difficult to see unless they are using appropriate lighting and wearing reflective clothing.

Animals

- Approach horse riders with special care. You must slow down, and pass giving them as much room as possible. Horses can be frightened by the sudden appearance of a vehicle, but it is more often the engine noise that spooks them.
- As you pass a horse, keep your speed down and your engine quiet. If you scare the horse by revving the engine, it may throw the rider into the road in front of you.
- Look out for animals in the road. In residential areas, you are more likely to have pets running out into the road, while in rural areas sheep and cattle can be a problem. Some areas may have deer in woodland areas, ducks and geese near the village pond or wild ponies. Be alert for clues of animals around, such as horse manure or sheep droppings in the road, eyes reflecting in your headlights at night, or signs for riding lessons next to the road.

> **TIP**
> Always slow down when you suspect there may be animals around. Remember, you do not emergency stop for animals, so if you want to avoid killing them, you must give yourself time to see them earlier.

It is important to recognise signs that warn you of more vulnerable road users

Other learner drivers

• The presence of other learner drivers often requires you to show more consideration, too. As a learner yourself, you will understand some of the problems learner drivers can have – they may not be as fast when moving away from junctions, they may miss seeing hazards until the last moment and then react suddenly and dramatically, or they might signal one thing and do another. Be patient with learners.

Other vehicles

• Emergency vehicles must always take priority on the road. If you hear a siren, look to see where the source is. Flashing lights of blue, red or green, or flashing main-beam lights will identify the vehicle. Try to anticipate where the vehicle may wish to go, and take appropriate action to let it pass. This usually involves pulling over to the side of the road and stopping. If you are in a right-hand lane, pull over to the right so that the vehicle can pass down the middle. You may only go as far as is necessary to make adequate space, and you must take great care. After the vehicle has passed, take care when returning to your normal position.

• Buses and public transport vehicles should be given preferential treatment. Always let them out

from a stop when they signal, and in meeting situations (see Section 8), try to let them through first if possible. Be careful near bus or tram stops, as pedestrians may step out from behind the vehicle, or be running to get on.

• Look out for vehicles displaying flashing amber lights. These warn of slow-moving or broken down vehicles. Flashing amber lights may be displayed by vehicles such as motorway maintenance trucks, vehicles surveying the road, gritters, diggers, recovery vehicles or JCBs.

• As you approach, there may be a queue building up around the vehicle, or it may be obstructing part of the road. Slow down and look out for workmen or operators who may be near by.

• Give plenty of space to large vehicles, such as lorries and wagons. Being much heavier, they are more difficult to stop or manoeuvre and, being longer, they require more room to turn. You may be behind a lorry in the right-hand lane which is signalling left.

• Whenever you see such conflicting signals from a large vehicle, hold back and give them room. In this case, the lorry is going to turn left but needs to use the whole width of the road in order to get around. Remember to allow room for lorries to emerge from a side road – they may need to swing out across the centre line.

Hierarchy of road users

The idea of the hierarchy of road users is to give those road users most at risk in the event of a collision priority. The road users most likely to be injured in the event of a collision are pedestrians, cyclists, horse riders and motorcyclists, with children, older adults and disabled people being more at risk. But this doesn't mean that these groups can behave how they like; all adults should behave responsibly.

- You should discuss this with your driving instructor so you understand the concept and what you need to do.
- Be sure to read the relevant section in *The Highway Code*.

Practice plan

It is not really possible to deliberately practise dealing with vulnerable road users – you must deal with each occasion as it arises. Try to time some practice sessions to coincide with school start or finish times. Make sure you drive through busy shopping streets to get experience of pedestrian activity. Otherwise, it is pretty much pot-luck what you will come across. Simply driving for as many hours as you can fit in will maximise your chances of meeting the widest variety of vulnerable road users.

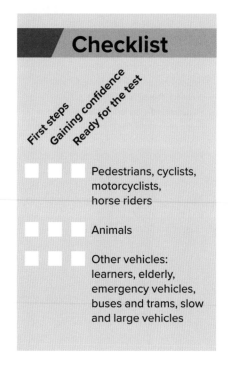

Checklist

First steps   Gaining confidence   Ready for the test

☐	☐	☐	Pedestrians, cyclists, motorcyclists, horse riders
☐	☐	☐	Animals
☐	☐	☐	Other vehicles: learners, elderly, emergency vehicles, buses and trams, slow and large vehicles

1

Motorcyclists are often less visible than other road users.

Complete this well-known phrase

Think once, think twice, think b__ __ __.

_____

2

What is the minimum amount of clearance you should give a cyclist or motorcyclist?

Answer _____

_____

_____

3

If you see a pedestrian at a zebra crossing or pelican crossing carrying a white stick, do you think...

Tick the correct box

1 They have difficulty walking? ☐

2 They are visually impaired? ☐

4

Which of the following statements are true?

On approach to traffic lights you should...

Tick the appropriate boxes

1 Speed up to get through before they change ☐

2 Be ready to stop ☐

3 Look for pedestrians ☐

4 Sound your horn to urge pedestrians to cross quickly ☐

_____

5

Certain groups of road users are particularly vulnerable at night.

Name two of them

1 _____

2 _____

VEHICLE CHECKS

You will be asked two vehicle safety questions as part of your Driving Test. One will be a 'Tell me...' question, at the start of the test, and one will be a 'Show me...' question, to be carried out while you are driving. There are 14 possible 'Tell me...' questions and seven possible 'Show me...' questions. It is important that you are sure your vehicle is safe and roadworthy, so carry out regular safety checks as standard practice.

How to do it

The following detailed instructions for checks should be applicable for most cars, but it is essential that you look in the handbook for your own car to check the details.

LEGAL REQUIREMENTS
Annexe 6 of *The Highway Code* deals with vehicle maintenance, safety and security.

'TELL ME' QUESTIONS:

For most of these questions, you will be expected to explain how you would carry out the check, but you won't be expected to perform it. The exception will be questions in which the examiner will ask you to open the bonnet; you should know how to do so and be able to identify the relevant components.

1. **'Tell me how you would check that the brakes are working before starting a journey.'**

Pumping the brake pedal when the engine is off should make the pedal very stiff. When the engine is started, the pedal should return to normal and should not feel spongy or slack. If this check is passed, perform a rolling brake check: as soon as you start off, brake to a stop. The car should stop smoothly and in a straight line. If the pedal feels spongy or slack, the brake fluid is leaking or too low. If the car shudders as it stops, there is a problem with the brake discs or pads. If the car pulls to one side as you brake, one of the brake circuits has failed. If any of these happen, don't drive the car.

2. **'Tell me where you would find the information for the recommended tyre pressures for this car and how you should check the pressures.'**

The information for the tyre pressures can be found in the handbook for the car, and on some makes of car it can also be found on the information label inside the little door that covers the petrol filler cap. On other makes, this label may be found on the open edge of the driver's door.

To check the tyre pressures, you would use a reliable tyre pressure gauge. Remove the tyre valve cap and press the gauge onto the valve. Hold it there for a second or two and read off the pressure from the digital readout or sliding scale (depending on the type of gauge you are using). Tyre pressures should be taken when the tyres are cold, as warm tyres will give a higher reading. Don't forget to check the spare tyre too.

3. Tell me how you'd make sure your head restraint is correctly adjusted so it provides the best protection in the event of a crash.

Adjust your head restraint so that the rigid part is about the height of your eyes or the top of your ears, and as close to the back of your head as is comfortable. Not all vehicles have adjustable head restraints.

4. 'Tell me how you'd check the tyres to ensure that they have sufficient tread depth and that their general condition is safe to use on the road.'

First check the general condition. The tyres should have no cuts or bulges in the tyre wall and should not look flat or under-inflated. The tread depth must be no less than 1.6mm across the central three-quarters of the width of the tyre and around the entire circumference. Use a tyre tread-depth gauge or feel for the marker bumps inside the main tread. If the main surface of the tyre is level with the bump, you need new tyres.

5. 'Tell me how you'd check that the headlights and tail lights are working. You don't need to exit the vehicle.'

Put the key in the ignition and turn it until the dashboard lights come on. Operate the light switch, turning it fully clockwise. Walk around the vehicle and look carefully at each light. You should see two bulbs illuminated on the headlights. In daylight, shade the rear light cluster with your hands to see the tail lights. Turn the lights off again.

6. Tell me how you'd know if there was a problem with your anti-lock braking system.

Put the key in the ignition and turn it until the dashboard lights come on. If there is a fault with the anti-lock braking system you should see a warning light. On most vehicles this will involve the letters 'ABS' within a circle.

7. 'Tell me how you'd check the direction indicators are working. You don't need to exit the vehicle.'

Again turn the key in the ignition, and indicate left. Get out and check that all three indicator lights (front, side and back) are flashing. Indicate right and check again.

TIP

Do not use the hazard warning light switch. This does allow you to check both sides in one go, but it doesn't tell you if the indicator stalk is working properly.

8. 'Tell me how you would check that the brake lights are working on this car.'

Turn the ignition on and operate the brake pedal. Ask a passenger to check if the lights are working. If you are alone, make use of reflections in shop windows or park close to a wall or garage door and look in the main mirror for three distinct pools of red light (some makes of car may have only two).

9. 'Tell me how you'd check the power-assisted steering is working before starting a journey.'

Check that the gear lever is in neutral and the handbrake is on. With two fingers of your left hand, pull down firmly on the steering wheel strut until it will no longer move. Maintain that pressure on the wheel as you start the engine. If the power assistance is working, the wheel will suddenly move as the engine starts.

10. Tell me how you'd switch on the rear fog light(s) and explain when you'd use it/them. You don't need to exit the vehicle.

Turn on the ignition and dipped headlights if necessary, then operate the switch for the rear fog lights. Check that the warning light is on. You should only use rear fog lights when visibility is at less than 100m, and turn them off again when visibility returns.

11. Tell me how you'd switch your headlight from dipped to main beam and explain how you'd know the main beam is on.

Turn on the ignition and dipped headlights if necessary, then switch to main beam using either the left stalk switch or a switch in the dashboard console. Check that the main beam warning light is on. You should only use the main beam when driving on empty, unlit roads during the hours of darkness, and must switch them off as soon as you see an oncoming vehicle.

Three questions concern items located in the engine compartment, so you must know how to open the bonnet of the car. Many cars have a lever in the driver's compartment that releases the bonnet. A catch below the bonnet itself is normally operated to raise the bonnet fully. For some cars, to open the bonnet you may also need to use a key.

In any car, you'll usually find the prop for the bonnet on the left-hand edge of the compartment. It fits into the two holes on the left underside of the bonnet.

12. 'Open the bonnet and tell me how you'd check that the engine has sufficient oil.'

At the front of the engine block, you will see a small yellow plastic loop handle. This is the dipstick. Pull the dipstick out, wipe it clean with a rag and push it back into the hole. Pull it out again and look to see where the oil level is showing. It should be between the two notches at the lower end of the stick. If the level is too low, you would top up the oil through the oil filler cap located on the top of the engine. Add a little oil at a time and keep checking the level until it reaches the upper notch. Only ever check the oil level when the engine is cold – the oil is dispersed when the engine has been running.

13. 'Open the bonnet and tell me how you'd check that the engine has sufficient engine coolant.'

In most cars the engine coolant reservoir is a big translucent plastic bottle, probably on the left of the engine as you face it. The fluid in it is usually pink, orange or green, but can be almost any bright, fluorescent colour. The bright colour warns you that the fluid, containing anti-freeze, is poisonous. On the side of the bottle facing you, you will see two lines – the maximum and minimum marks. The level of fluid must be between the two lines. If the level is too low you must wait for the engine to cool down before topping up the bottle with water.

14. 'Open the bonnet and tell me how you'd check that you have a safe level of hydraulic brake fluid.'

In most cars, the brake fluid reservoir is located at the rear of the engine compartment – check the handbook for your car to ensure you know where to find it. Again, there are two lines marked – maximum and minimum – and the level must be between the two lines. As the brake fluid is clear, it can be difficult to see the level. Tap the bottle to make the fluid move, making it easier to see. If the brake fluid level is low, top it up using the correct type of brake fluid and take the car to a garage to see why the level has dropped – you may have a leak somewhere that needs fixing.

'SHOW ME' QUESTIONS:

These questions will be asked during your test, while you are driving.

1. **When it's safe to do so, can you show me how you'd wash and clear the rear windscreen?**

2. **When it's safe to do so, can you show me how you'd wash and clean the front windscreen?**

3. **When it's safe to do so, can you show me how you'd switch on your dipped headlights?**

4. **When it's safe to do so, can you show me how you'd set the rear demister?**

5. **'When it's safe to do so, can you show me how you'd operate the horn?'**

TIP
You do not need the ignition on for this test – the horn should work at any time. This is in case you are out of the car with the key and your passenger sees that they are in danger from a moving vehicle.

6. **When it's safe to do so, can you show me how you'd demist the front windscreen?**

7. **When it's safe to do so, can you show me how you'd open and close the side window?**

REGULAR MAINTENANCE

It is vital that your vehicle is properly maintained and roadworthy. Not only must you ensure that your vehicle is safe to use on the road, but you will be less likely to suffer the inconvenience of a breakdown if you regularly perform a few essential checks.

FLOWERY CHECK

You should carry out this check at least every week, and before any major journey.

Fuel – make sure you have enough for your journey, or at least enough to reach the next petrol station.

Lights – check all lights, indicators and brake lights.

Oil – check your engine oil level as described at the beginning of this section.

Water – check the levels of your engine coolant and windscreen wash.

Electrics – check all electrical features: horn, windscreen wipers, etc.

Rubber – check your tyres for damage and wear and tear, and check the tyre pressures, remembering to check the spare wheel at the same time. Also check the windscreen wiper blades for wear, and replace if necessary.

Yourself – make sure that you are not unfit to drive because of tiredness, drink, drugs, medicines or other pressures.

As you perform the FLOWERY check, make replacements or repair any faults you find, and top up any fluid levels as necessary. As you walk around the car, check for any damage to the bodywork.

DAILY CHECKS

Make a visual inspection of the car every day, paying special attention to the tyres, lights and external bodywork, and glass.

Walk around the car before getting in for the first time each day. Check that the tyres are not flat, and that you can see no obvious damage to the tyre walls. Make sure the bodywork and glass is intact and, as soon as you get in, check all the lights are working properly.

Every time you start the engine for the first time that day, carry out a brake check (see page 223) – that alone could save your own or someone else's life.

CLEAN AND TIDY

Keeping your car clean will allow you to spot any potential problems as early as possible. For example, if your wheels are caked in mud, you may not notice the nail sticking in the tread.

Keep the glass (windscreen, side windows and mirrors) clean at all times – you must always be able to see clearly. Clean windscreens reduce the dazzle at night, and are less prone to misting in rain. Keep suitable cloths handy for use in the car, but only use them when you are properly parked.

Secure any loose items inside your car. Use the glovebox, door and seat pockets or the boot to safely stow anything you may need to carry. Loose items can become lethal missiles in the event of sudden braking or a collision. Make sure that the foot-wells are kept empty, and don't store anything under the seats. When you brake, such items could slide forward and prevent proper use of the pedals.

Make sure any pets are properly secured in the rear of the car. Do not allow them to roam freely around the passenger compartment, as they can distract you while you drive. For maximum safety, have either a pet cage or safety bars fitted, so that animals are kept separately from the main compartment. This is not only safer for your pet in the event of a collision (they will not be thrown around), but also prevents them from becoming a potentially lethal missile.

Practice plan

Periodically check that you remember how to perform all the checks. Try to do at least one pair of questions (one 'show me' and one 'tell me') every time you go out in the car. When practising, do the checks for real – don't just 'tell'. You will find it easier to explain if you have actually performed the checks yourself.

Checklist

First steps	Gaining confidence	Ready for the test	
☐	☐	☐	Open bonnet
☐	☐	☐	Engine oil
☐	☐	☐	Engine coolant
☐	☐	☐	Brake fluid
☐	☐	☐	Windscreen wash
☐	☐	☐	Tyre pressures
☐	☐	☐	Tyre condition and tread depth
☐	☐	☐	Head- and tail lights
☐	☐	☐	Indicators
☐	☐	☐	Brake lights
☐	☐	☐	Footbrake
☐	☐	☐	Handbrake
☐	☐	☐	Power-assisted steering
☐	☐	☐	Horn
☐	☐	☐	FLOWERY check
☐	☐	☐	Clean and tidy

1

With which of these statements do you agree?

Tick the correct box

1 Allowing the fuel gauge to drop too low is bad for the engine. ☐

2 In modern cars the fuel level makes little difference. ☐

_____

2

What do you put into the engine to lubricate the moving parts?

Answer _____

_____

_____

_____

3

How frequently should you check your oil level?

Tick the correct box

1 Once a month ☐

2 Once a year ☐

3 Every time you fill up with fuel ☐

4

The engine is often cooled by a mixture of w__ __ __ __ and a__ __ __ __ f__ __ __ __ __.

Some engines are a__ __ cooled.

Complete the sentence

_____

5

How frequently should you test your brakes?

Tick the correct box

1 Daily ☐

2 Monthly ☐

3 Weekly ☐

4 When I use them ☐

_____

6

Incorrectly adjusted headlamps can cause d__ __ __ __ __ to other road users.

Complete the sentence

7

All headlamps, indicators and brake lights should be kept in good working order. It is also important that they are kept c__ __ __ __ .

Fill in the missing word

_____

8

Tyres should be checked for u__ __ __ __ __ wear and tyre walls for b__ __ __ __ __ and c__ __ __.

Complete the sentence

_____

9

The legal requirement for tread depth is not less than ...

Tick the correct box

1 1.4mm   ☐

2 1.6mm   ☐

3 2mm   ☐

10

What should you do if your brakes feel slack or spongy?

Answer _____

_____

_____

_____

11

Vehicle breakdowns could result from...

Fill in the missing words

1 N__ __ __ __ __ __ of the vehicle

2 Lack of r__ __ __ __ __ __ c__ __ __ __ __

3 Little or no p__ __ __ __ __ __ __ __ __ __ maintenance

4 A__ __ __ __ of the vehicle

AUTOMATICS

We have now covered the basic skills required for controlling the vehicle. but we also need to consider the use of cars with automatic gearboxes. Even if you drive a car with a manual gearbox, you still need to read this section, as the Theory Test includes questions relating to the use of automatics. Whether driving an automatic car or not, you need to know the major differences between automatic and manual transmissions and how to control a vehicle with an automatic gear box.

How to do it

Common features
Automatic gearboxes come in many different versions, so we will first consider the common features before looking at optional features you may find on some cars. For a thorough understanding of how the gearbox on your car should be used, please refer to the manufacturer's handbook.

Vehicles with automatic transmission do not have a clutch pedal. Gears are changed automatically when the car senses a change in speed or load on the engine – for example, going uphill. It is possible to over-ride the sensors and force the car to select a specific gear (so-called 'locked' gears), but for most driving situations the automatic gearbox will select the most appropriate gear for the speed you are travelling.

The gear selector
Almost all automatics have a gear selector, though there may be minor differences between various models. The layout is usually as follows:

P – Park. This setting locks the transmission and must only be used when the car is stationary.

R – Reverse

N – Neutral. As in a manual gearbox, this setting allows you to have the engine running but with no connection to the wheels.

LEGAL REQUIREMENTS
If you pass your Driving Test in a car with automatic transmission, you are only licensed to drive automatics. If you later want to drive a car with a manual gearbox, you must first pass the test in a manual. There is only one specific reference to automatics in *The Highway Code* – rule 252. All other rules and advice apply as for a manual car.

D – Drive. This setting selects the fully automatic mode. The car will automatically select the best gear to use for the speed or load on the engine.

3 – Third gear
(not on all models)

2 – Second gear

1 – First gear

The selectable gears 1, 2 and 3 force the transmission to use the selected or a lower gear – the car will not use a higher gear than the one chosen. This is useful when going down steep hills, where you normally use a lower gear.

There may be a lever or switch on the selector itself that you must operate in order to move the selector. Again, details of the particular set-up in your car will be found in the manual.

MOVING OFF
Creep
Automatics are deliberately designed to 'creep' forward without the need for any pressure on the accelerator. Because of this, it is essential that, when stationary, you either keep your right foot firmly on the brake pedal, or you apply the handbrake.

Preparation
Although most automatics have a cut-off switch that will not allow you to start the engine while in gear, check that the selector is in park or neutral and that the handbrake is fully applied when you first enter the vehicle. As an additional safety feature before starting the engine, many cars require you to press firmly on the footbrake to prevent 'creep'. Select the Drive position using the gear selector and release the handbrake.

Observation
Check all around the car, finishing by looking into the blind spot over your right shoulder.

Manoeuvre
Take your foot off the footbrake. The car will creep forward – even on a hill, provided it is not too steep. The car will continue to creep at this speed until you apply some pressure to the gas pedal. If you are performing a manoeuvre, such as a turn in the road, do not use the accelerator, but simply control the speed using the brake pedal. The same applies whether you are going forwards or reversing.

If you intend to drive on normally, as you start to move gently squeeze the gas pedal. Maintain a steady pressure as you get to the correct rate of acceleration. The gear box will automatically change up through the gears for you.

Kick-down
If you need to accelerate more quickly – for example when joining a road with a faster speed limit – you can use the 'kick-down' device. This feature, common to all automatics, allows you to over-ride the automatic selection of gears and forces the transmission to stay in the lower gears for longer. This gives you much greater acceleration than normal.

As the name implies, you press down sharply on the gas pedal. Some models of automatic gearboxes have a definite 'click' on the accelerator pedal when you press down like this, while others just sense the rapid movement and change down for you. Keep the pedal all the way down until you reach your desired speed.

When you have reached the speed you want, ease back off the gas and the car will automatically return to normal drive and select the most appropriate gear.

Slowing and stopping

Automatic gear boxes do not respond as quickly to easing off the gas, and so engine braking is reduced. To slow down, transfer your right foot from the gas pedal to the brake. Because of the reduced engine braking, you must brake sooner and more progressively than in a manual car. The transmission will automatically work its way down through the gears as you slow down, so that you are always in the correct gear. This is a great help at all types of junctions and in any situation where you need to slow down, as you can concentrate on observations and safety rather than on changing gear.

As you come to a stop, keep your foot on the footbrake.

TIP
The car will not stall, even if you have stopped very quickly as in an emergency stop.

Parking and waiting

Under normal driving conditions, you would apply the handbrake whenever a pause becomes a wait. If you are to be stationary for more than a few seconds, apply the handbrake firmly. This allows you to release the footbrake so that your brake lights do not dazzle the driver behind you.

If you are parking, apply the handbrake and select the Park position before releasing the footbrake. Just before you intend to drive on, reapply the footbrake and only then select Drive again.

Using the handbrake is even more important on automatics than manuals, as the car will move away if the selector is in Drive. Accidentally touching the gas pedal can be enough for the car to move, even with the handbrake fully on, so when you stop, keep your foot on the footbrake until you have selected Park or Neutral.

Additional features

Under normal driving conditions, the use of Drive and the 'kick-down' feature will give adequate control. There are a number of situations where you may need to use additional features. Note that some cars with a manual gearbox also have some of these features.

Hill starts – on a steep hill, creep may be insufficient to get you moving. Some automatics have a feature that will prevent roll back, but more usually you should use the following routine:

* With the handbrake fully on, very gently apply a little pressure to the gas pedal. You will feel the nose of the car start to rise slightly.
* When it is safe to drive on, release the handbrake.
* Let the car creep forward slightly, before gently squeezing down the gas pedal.

On very steep hills, you may wish to cover the footbrake with your left foot, but only use it if the car starts to roll backwards.

Driving downhill – under normal conditions, automatics will select a higher gear when you ease off the gas pedal. If you are approaching a downhill section, you can over-ride this by using the selector to choose one of the locked gear positions – 1, 2 or 3. This will force the transmission to select the chosen gear, giving you more engine braking and lessening the need to brake.

Cornering – for similar reasons, cornering needs to be approached more carefully in an automatic car. As you ease off the gas on the approach to a bend, the transmission may select a higher gear. This could cause you to corner faster than you had intended. To avoid this, slow down as you approach and gently accelerate just before starting the turn. This will encourage the automatic gearbox to select a lower gear for the corner. If your car has the locked third gear position, you could use it to prevent the selection of a higher gear on bendy roads.

Snow or ice – some automatics have a 'snow button' for use in icy conditions or in any situation where traction control is paramount, such as on gravel or wet grass. This button forces the transmission to select a higher gear than normal, reducing the amount of torque at the drive wheels and thus the likelihood of wheel-spin. If your car has not got a snow button, you can achieve a similar effect by selecting the locked 2 or 3 positions.

Economical driving – some automatics have an economy mode button that causes the transmission to select the higher gears at lower revs than normal. This saves petrol but at the expense of performance – you will not be able to accelerate as quickly. Use this mode where you are unlikely to need quick acceleration, or as an alternative to the snow button in icy or frosty conditions.

Sports – some automatics have a 'sports' button. When in sports mode, the gears will change at much higher revs than normal, giving much more power and acceleration, but at the expense of fuel consumption. Sports mode is really only suitable for track days, or occasional use when you need to accelerate quickly, such as joining motorways and dual carriageways, or overtaking. Even then, 'kick-down' is the preferred method of gaining the extra power required.

Manoeuvring – because 'creep' will move the car slowly, it is likely that you will not need to use the gas when manoeuvring at slow speed. If manoeuvring on a hill or where the road has a marked camber, you may find a little gas will keep the car moving slowly enough. In such situations, it is permissible to use your left foot on the brake pedal at the same time as holding the gas with your right foot. This is not a technique you should ever use at any other time – it is safer to use only your right foot for both accelerator and brake when driving normally.

It is not necessary to use the handbrake during the turn in the road manoeuvre. Examiners are happy for you to keep the car stationary using only the footbrake, as you would normally keep the footbrake on except when in Park or Neutral. It is rare for examiners to ask you to perform a hill start in an automatic, as they know that the car will do almost all the work for you.

Practice plan

First steps
Follow the suggestions given in the practice plans for all sections in the same way, but making the necessary changes to account for the automatic gearbox.

Start with simple moving away, stopping and speed control. Remember to use the foot and handbrakes properly.

Gaining confidence
Practise the use of 'kick-down' and the locked gears when accelerating and going downhill. Experiment with any additional modes available on your car, such as the snow button or economy setting. Check the dashboard display to see if it tells you what selection is currently active.

Practise the manoeuvres as they arise in the natural progression of your lessons. You will almost certainly find these much easier than in a manual car, where controlling the speed by clutch control is a major consideration.

Ready for the test

Remember that for all the situations detailed in this book where MSM/PSL or other routines are used, you still need to follow the routine – only the specific details of changing or selecting gears will differ. You will have a natural advantage over manual car drivers, as they need to spend a significant amount of time considering and carrying out gear changes. The speed phase of MSM/PSL becomes much easier: just use the footbrake or gas to get to the appropriate speed.

This does not mean that you can delay the MSM/PSL routine in an automatic, but it does mean that you are likely to find it easier to control the car and have more time to concentrate on steering, observations and driving smoothly.

Only when you are completely comfortable with the basic features of the automatic gearbox should you try the more advanced settings such as sports mode.

Checklist

First steps · Gaining confidence · Ready for the test

- The gear selector
- Moving off: level and on hills
- Accelerating and 'kick-down'
- Slowing and stopping
- Use of hand- and footbrakes
- Use of Park and Neutral
- Creep
- Use of locked gears
- Cornering
- Manoeuvring

Additional features if fitted

- Snow button
- Economy mode
- Sports mode

1

Cars fitted with automatic transmission select the gear depending on the road speed and the load on the engine. They therefore have no c___ ___ ___ ___ ___ pedal.

Fill in the missing word

_____

2

The advantages of an automatic car are...

1 _____
_____
2 _____
_____

_____

3

The gear selector has the same function as a manual selector, but what function do each of the following have?

P	Park_____ _____
R	Reverse_____ _____
N	Neutral_____ _____
D	Drive_____ _____
3	3rd_____ _____
2	2nd_____ _____
1	1st_____ _____

4

Automatic cars have a device called a kickdown. Is its function...

Tick the correct box

1 To select a higher gear? ☐

2 To select a lower gear manually? ☐

3 To provide quick acceleration when needed? ☐

_____

5

When driving an automatic car, would you select a lower gear...

Tick the appropriate boxes	YES	NO
1 To control speed when going down a steep hill?	☐	☐
2 To slow the car down in normal driving?	☐	☐
3 When going uphill?	☐	☐
4 To overtake, in certain circumstances?	☐	☐
5 When manoeuvring?	☐	☐
6 Before stopping?	☐	☐

_____

6

An automatic car has two foot pedals, the foot-brake and the accelerator.

For normal driving, which foot would you use...

1 For the brake?
Answer _____

2 For the accelerator?
Answer _____

7

When you are driving an automatic car, using one foot to control both pedals is preferable to using both the left and the right foot. Why?

Answer _____

_____

_____

8

Some cars with automatic transmission have a tendency to 'creep'.

Which gears allow the car to creep?

Answer _____

_____

_____

9

When driving an automatic car, would you use the handbrake...

Tick the correct box

1 More than in a manual car? ☐

2 The same? ☐

3 Less? ☐

10

In which position should the gear selector be when you are starting the engine?

Answer _____

or _____

11

As you approach a bend, an automatic car will sometimes change up because there is less pressure on the accelerator.

What should you do to prevent this happening?

Tick the correct box

1 Slow down before the bend and accelerate gently as you turn. ☐

2 Brake as you go round the bend. ☐

3 Brake and accelerate at the same time. ☐

THE TEST

LEGAL REQUIREMENTS

You will need to take your valid provisional photocard licence and your Theory Test pass certificate with you to the test. If you have kept it, take your appointment confirmation letter as well, just in case there is a problem with the computers. Don't worry if you haven't got this – it is not essential.

If you are taking your test in your own car, you should also take a valid insurance certificate for that vehicle with you. You must also provide an extra rear-view mirror for the examiner's use, and ensure that the passenger seat is secure and has a working seatbelt and head restraint. Make sure that L-plates are displayed without obscuring the front or rear windows.

If the weather is particularly bad on the day of your test, you should telephone the DVSA to check whether tests are going ahead at your Test Centre (contact the DVSA on 0300 200 1122). If your test is cancelled, you will be offered another appointment as soon as possible.

If you are unable to find any of the required documents, telephone the DVSA as soon as possible and seek their advice. If you are still missing documents on the last working day before your test, telephone again to make sure the necessary arrangements have been made. On the day of your test, you should arrive about ten minutes early and speak to an examiner to make sure they have received the necessary paperwork.

How to do it

PREPARATION
It is sensible to book a driving lesson before your test. Most instructors will book this in automatically when you notify them of the time of your test. Make sure you have all the required documents with you and show them to your instructor before you leave home.

Arrange to arrive at the Test Centre at least ten minutes before your appointed test time, as you may have to wait to park and you may want time to mentally prepare yourself.

Make sure your car is secure and parked in the correct place before finding the test waiting room. Have your documents ready for the examiner.

THE START
The examiner will come out and call your name. They will ask you to read and sign the insurance and residency declarations while they check your documents are in order.

They will ask you if you would like to take someone with you on your test, usually your driving instructor, to sit in the back of the car and observe, but not take part in the test.

The examiner will then ask you to lead the way to your vehicle. Remember, they don't know which your car is, so you will have to lead the way.

Eyesight test
As you walk out, the examiner will ask you to stop somewhere to do the eyesight test. You must be able to read a new-style plate at 20m or an old-style number plate at a distance of 20.5m. If you wear glasses or contact lenses to read the number plate then you must wear them when driving. If there is any problem with your eyesight the test will not go ahead.

At the car
As you continue towards the car, the examiner may offer to explain what the test will involve.

The first part of the test will be a vehicle check, or 'Tell Me...' question. The examiner will ask one of the fourteen questions from Section 21.

Later in the test, while driving, you will also be asked one 'Show Me...' question – this will be one of the seven questions indicated in Section 21.

TIP
Remember, for the 'Show Me...' question you must physically demonstrate the answer, not just explain it verbally.

The examiner will then usually ask you to get in and prepare yourself, saying that they will join you in a moment. Get in and perform a brief cockpit drill. The examiner knows you have just driven to the Test Centre, so they are not expecting you to alter anything. They will expect you to make a quick visual check that everything is as you left it and to put your seatbelt on.

When they join you in the car, they will explain what they would like you to do:

'During the test I would like you to follow the road ahead at all times, unless signs or markings indicate otherwise, or I ask you to make a turn, which I will do in good time. When you are ready, move off.'

This is your cue to check the handbrake is on and the gear lever in neutral, before starting the engine.

THE TEST DRIVE

To pass the test, you must commit no more than fifteen driving faults, and none of these must be serious or dangerous. A driving fault is anything that is not correct. Some driving faults may be of no consequence and the examiner will not record them. A serious fault is one that is potentially dangerous and could cause other road users to take action. A dangerous fault is one where you cause actual danger to yourself or other road users.

The test will last around 40 minutes and will cover a variety of roads, including where possible rural and urban roads and dual carriageways. The route you follow will almost certainly include roundabouts, crossroads, pedestrian crossings and roads through residential, shopping and country areas.

The routes are planned to include the widest range of driving possible in that area and to give a consistent standard of testing across the whole country. Your driving instructor will have taken you around most of the areas you are likely to use in your test.

TIP
Don't worry if you find yourself in an area you have never seen before. Drive as you have been taught, and make sure you look ahead and plan for what you see.

The manoeuvres

During the test you will be asked to perform one of the manoeuvres you have practised with your instructor. These are chosen from:

- Bay park – either reversing into a bay or forward parking into a bay. Your examiner will tell you which to do. Reversing into a bay must be done in the Test Centre car park at the very beginning or end of the test (some centres do not have the facilities to ask for this exercise), but forward parking in a bay can be done in any car park.
- Parallel park.
- Pull up on the right, reverse for two car lengths and rejoin traffic.

In addition, you may be asked to demonstrate the emergency stop exercise. This does not count as one of the manoeuvres and is asked on approximately one third of all tests.

On several occasions, you will be asked to pull over and park on the left. This may be so that the examiner can give you instructions for one of the exercises, or they may then ask you to move off again immediately. You may be asked to stop on a hill or close to a parked vehicle. These stops are to check that you can move off safely and under control normally, on a hill or at an angle.

Navigation

If you come to a junction or roundabout where the examiner has given no instruction to turn, you should follow the road directly ahead.

TIP
Always plan to follow the road ahead unless the examiner tells you otherwise.

If there are road signs or markings indicating that you must proceed in a certain direction, make sure you obey them.

You may ask the examiner to repeat the instructions or question them if you are unsure. The test is a test of your driving ability, not navigational ability, so don't worry if you have to ask for confirmation of the directions. If you get confused between left and right, ask the examiner to use additional hand signals along with the verbal directions. This problem is much more common than you might think, especially under test conditions, so don't feel embarrassed. If you do happen to take a wrong turn, don't worry, the examiner will simply direct you back to the route or stop you and ask you to turn around.

Independent driving

The examiner will ask you to drive for about 20 minutes – about half of the test – without specific directions to see if you can drive without someone giving you instructions. The examiner will confirm the directions if you ask for a reminder. During this time they will continue to assess your driving skills. Your driving instructor will help you practise this skill before your test.

It is also likely that you will be asked to follow directions from a sat nav for part of this time. This will be provided and set up by your examiner, and you will not be required to touch it at any time. Not every test will involve a sat nav – one in five driving tests will ask you to follow road signs instead.

END OF THE TEST

At the end of the test, when you have parked at the Test Centre, the examiner will tell you that it is the end of the test. They may take a few moments to complete the form and check their adding up, and will then tell you whether you have passed or not. If you have passed, they will ask for your licence and will complete the necessary paperwork before offering to de-brief you on your performance. If you have not passed, they will offer you a de-brief there and then, and will ask if you would like a form to re-book your test.

If they did not accompany you on your test you should ask if your instructor can listen to the de-brief, as you are likely to be either too elated or too dejected to pay much attention to what they have to say. The examiner will also give you a Test Report Form, which is a copy of their markings, a sheet explaining the marks and a guide to the report form.

If you have passed, well done. If you haven't passed, you may need some more tuition before trying again, so make sure you discuss this with your instructor. Most fail because of mistakes which are either due to inexperience or nerves, or a mixture of both. Inexperience and nerves can both be improved by practice, so make sure you take the time to practise as much as possible.

The Test Report Form and the examiner's de-brief will help you correct your mistakes for the next time and will also guide you as to how much extra tuition you are likely to need.

If you need to re-take your test, you must wait a minimum of 10 working days before you are allowed to sit the test again. You can actually book the next test immediately, but you will not be allocated an appointment for at least two weeks.

1

There are many myths and misunderstandings surrounding the driving test.

Are the following true or false?

Tick the correct boxes   **True**   **False**

1 The driving test is designed to see whether I can drive around a test route without making any mistakes. ☐ ☐

2 The driving test is designed to see whether I can drive safely under various traffic conditions. ☐ ☐

3 I do not need to know any of *The Highway Code*. ☐ ☐

4 The examiner has a set allocation of passes each week. ☐ ☐

5 I may be expected to drive up to the maximum national speed limit, where appropriate. ☐ ☐

2

The length of the normal driving test is approximately...

Tick the correct box

1 60 minutes ☐

2 90 minutes ☐

3 40 minutes ☐

3

It is essential that you take both sections of your

p__ __ __ __ __ __ __ __ __ __
l__ __ __ __ __ __ to the test centre.

Fill in the missing words

_____

4

Before the practical part of your test, the examiner will test your eyesight. This is done by asking you to read a new-style number plate at a distance of...

Tick the correct box

1 30.5 metres (100 feet) ☐

2 20 metres (67 feet) ☐

3 40.5 metres (133 feet) ☐

5

What will happen if you fail your eyesight test?

Answer _____

_____

_____

6

The examiner will expect you to drive without making any mistakes.

Do you think this statement is true or false?

Tick the correct box   **True** ☐   **False** ☐

7

If, during the test, you do not understand what the examiner says to you, you would take a guess because you must not talk to him or her.

Is this statement true or false?

Tick the correct box **True** ☐ **False** ☐

8

While taking your driving test, you should drive...

Tick the correct box

1 Especially carefully, keeping about 5mph below the speed limit ☐

2 As you would normally drive with your instructor ☐

3 With confidence, keeping at or just over the speed limit, to show that you can really drive ☐

9

If you fail your test, what will the examiner do?

1 _____

_____

2 _____

_____

10

If you fail your test, you can take it again. Which of the following statements is correct?

Tick the correct box(es)

1 If you fail the test, you can apply straight away for another appointment. ☐

2 If you fail the test you have to wait a month before you can apply for another appointment. ☐

3 You can re-take your test, subject to appointment availability, any time. ☐

4 You have to wait 10 working days before you can re-take the test. ☐

11

When you have passed your driving test, what are you entitled to do?

1 _____

_____

2 _____

_____

12

I have within the last month passed my test.

Can I supervise a learner driver?

Tick the correct box **YES** ☐ **NO** ☐

AFTER THE TEST

Well done – you've passed!
You demonstrated to the examiner that you are safe to drive on the roads unaccompanied. However, it is worth remembering that you are still an inexperienced driver and statistics show that, unless you are very careful, this is the time you are most likely to have a collision. Now is the time to consider some further training.

Statistics show that newly qualified drivers are around ten times more likely to have a collision in the first two years of their driving career than in the whole of the remaining 60 years or so. One in five fatal car crashes involves a driver under the age of 25; 20 per cent of all drivers will crash during their first two years. This is why insurance premiums are so high when you start driving.

PASS PLUS

The Pass Plus scheme is designed to help you gain the valuable experience and skills to become a safer driver for life. Supported by participating insurance companies, Pass Plus aims to enable new drivers to:

- develop their existing skills, learn new skills, techniques and knowledge to enhance their driving
- improve the skills of anticipation and awareness
- understand how to reduce the risks of having a collision
- maintain a courteous and considerate attitude when driving on the road.

Drivers who successfully complete the course will be offered substantial discounts on their insurance premiums – usually a free one-year's no claims discount. This can amount to a 30% or more discount and far exceeds the cost of taking the course.

The course covers six modules and must be at least six hours long. The modules are:

- introduction and town driving
- all-weather driving
- out-of-town driving and rural roads
- night driving
- dual carriageways
- motorway driving.

While you will have covered most of these topics when learning to drive, on the Pass Plus course the emphasis is centred on a positive approach to driving. The focus on attitude and skills gives a different perspective on these topics and is designed to enhance your existing abilities and knowledge, rather than simply replicating them.

Once you have passed your test, talk to your instructor about taking the course.

TIP
Nearly all AA Driving School instructors are registered to teach Pass Plus.

MOTORWAY DRIVING

If you decide the Pass Plus course isn't for you, you could consider taking the motorway driving course, run by AA Driving School. While in theory there is very little difference between driving on a motorway or a dual carriageway, those differences are important, and in practice the experience can be quite daunting and intimidating.

The main difference is that there is an extra lane. Even a two-lane motorway differs from a dual carriageway in that it has a hard shoulder. This emergency lane is only to be used when a vehicle has broken down. It does, however, mean that there is always the possibility of vehicles pulling out from the hard shoulder when you are returning to the left-hand lane after overtaking. You must always take care when changing lanes, and on a motorway you must always signal your intent to change lanes.

Another difference is the breakdown procedure. On a motorway, you must use the hard shoulder only in an emergency. Stop as far to the left as you can and near an emergency telephone if possible. These are positioned along the hard shoulder about one mile apart. An arrow on the rear of the marker posts indicates the direction to the nearest phone. Turn on your hazard warning lights and, if it is dark, your sidelights. Exit your vehicle through the left-hand door and get your passengers clear, well back from the hard shoulder. If you have animals in the vehicle they must be left in it unless it is an emergency. If you do take them out, make sure they are kept under strict control.

Use the nearest emergency telephone to call for assistance. The call is free and will connect you directly to the police. Do not use your mobile phone to call for help unless you are unable to get to an emergency phone due to disability or injury. By using the emergency phones the police will be aware of your situation and will be able to pinpoint your location. If you must use a mobile, make sure you note the number of the nearest marker post. The police will call your breakdown organisation for you and, if you are a vulnerable motorist (for example, a woman travelling alone) will ensure a patrol car is sent to assist as soon as possible. Disabled drivers should have a help pennant.

Do not attempt even simple repairs, such as changing a wheel, at the side of motorway. If you have just had a puncture, the same debris could cause another vehicle to have one too, and they could lose control and run into you.

Smart motorways

Some UK motorways are now 'smart' motorways, which use technology to manage the flow of traffic. This includes opening the hard shoulder to traffic, and using electronic signs to close lanes or reduce speed limits as needed. If you are going to drive on a smart motorway, you should familiarise yourself with the advice given by Highways England on gov.uk/guidance/how-to-drive-on-a-smart-motorway.

TIP

Rules 253–274 of *The Highway Code* cover motorway driving. Rules 275–287 cover the procedures to follow if you break down or are involved in an incident.

DRIVE CONFIDENT

Drive Confident, a course run by AA Driving School, is for qualified drivers in need of refresher driver training to increase confidence on the road. The in-car sessions, either in your own car or an AA vehicle, include an assessment to identify your specific needs, followed by guided practice and coaching.

You won't need to sit a test at the end of the course – the sessions are simply about helping you become a more confident driver.

For further information visit theAA.com/driving-school

THE NEXT STEP

Having passed your test, you must now take care to drive as you have been taught. You will hear people saying, 'Now you've passed the test, you will learn to drive.' This is nonsense. You have learnt to drive and what you did to pass your test was the right way to drive. What they really mean is that, having passed your test, you will now gain experience.

The experience you gain in the first few months is the most valuable you will ever get. This is where, if you let it happen, you will pick up all the bad habits that will stay with you for the rest of your driving career. Avoid the bad habits, for they are just that – bad. You have learned the skills you need to be a safe driver, and you have learned the right way to execute those skills. Doing anything other than what you were taught is bad driving.

As for habits, these are what drivers generally rely on when they are no longer thinking. You cannot drive on habits. You must constantly think about what you are doing and why you are doing it. Concentrate on being aware of what is happening, assessing the situation, actively deciding and planning what to do and then executing that plan with skill and control. Driving is an activity – you must be actively involved, not a passive observer.

Well done and drive on safely.

1

Do you think that learning to drive ends with passing the test?

Tick the correct box   **YES** ☐ **NO** ☐

2

What knowledge and skills are not necessarily assessed in the present driving test?

List three

1 _____
_____

2 _____
_____

3 _____
_____

3

Which of these statements do you think best describes advanced driving?

Tick the correct box

1 Advanced driving is learning to handle your car to its maximum performance. ☐

2 Advanced driving is learning to drive defensively with courtesy and consideration to others. ☐

3 Advanced driving is learning to drive fast. ☐

4

Motorways are designed to enable traffic to travel faster in greater safety.

Compared to other roads, are they statistically...

Tick the correct box

1 Safer? ☐

2 Less safe? ☐

3 No different? ☐

5

Are the following groups allowed on the motorway?

Tick the correct boxes

1 Provisional licence holders supervised by a qualified driver ☐

2 Provisional licence holders supervised by an Approved Driving Instructor (ADI) ☐

3 Motor cycles over 50cc ☐

4 Pedestrians ☐

5 HGV learner drivers ☐

6 Newly qualified drivers with less than three months' experience ☐

7 Motor cycles under 125cc ☐

8 Cyclists ☐

6

On the motorway, if something falls from either your own or another vehicle, should you...

Tick the correct box

1 Flash your headlights to inform other drivers? ☐

2 Pull over, put your hazard warning lights on and quickly run on to the motorway to collect the object? ☐

3 Pull over on to the hard shoulder, use the emergency telephone to call the police? ☐

4 Flag another motorist down to get help? ☐

7

Which colour do you associate with motorway signs?

Tick the correct box

1 Black lettering on a white background ☐

2 White lettering on a green background ☐

3 White lettering on a blue background ☐

8

What is the most common cause of accidents on motorways?

Tick the correct box

1 Vehicles breaking down ☐

2 Drivers falling asleep ☐

3 Drivers travelling too fast, too close to the vehicle in front ☐

4 Fog ☐

9

Are the following statements true or false?

I can use the hard shoulder...

	True	False
Tick the correct boxes		
1 To take a short break	☐	☐
2 To stop and read a map	☐	☐
3 To allow the children to stretch their legs	☐	☐
4 To pull over in an emergency	☐	☐
5 To answer a phone call	☐	☐

Part 3:
Answers to Driving
Test Skills Questions

Section 1

Controls and cockpit drill

A1   **1** handbrake
         2 doors
         3 seat
         4 head restraint
         5 mirrors
         6 seat belt
A2   The foot-brake R
         The clutch L
         The accelerator R
A3   The handbrake E
         The driving mirrors D
         The gear lever F
         The clutch G
         The steering wheel A
         The foot-brake B
         The accelerator C
A4   gas
A5   **1** False. You will need one hand to
         change gear or use other controls.
         2 True
         3 False. The best position is quarter
         to three or ten to two.
         4 False. It is safest to feed the wheel
         through your hands.
         5 True
         6 True
A6   **B**
A7   The direction indicators B
         Dipped beam A
         Main beam D
         Rear fog lamp C
         Horn E
         Hazard lights F

Section 2

Moving off and stopping normally

A1   **A** 1
         B 5
         C 3
         D 2
         E 6
         F 4
         G 7
         H 8
         I 9

A2   **A** 1
         B 3
         C 2
         D 4
         E 6
         F 5
         G 8
         H 7
         I 9

Section 3

Clutch control and changing gear

A1   1st gear
A2   **A** 1
         B 3
         C 2
         D 4
         E 5
A3   5th, or 4th if the car has a 4-speed gear
         box
A4   **1** False. This will cause the engine
         to labour.
         2 False. It is good practice to use the
         brakes to slow the car down. Using the
         transmission causes wear and tear which
         can be very costly. Also, the brakes are
         more effective.
         3 False
         4 True
         5 False. It is good practice to miss out
         the unwanted gears and select the gear
         most appropriate to your road speed.
A5   **1**
A6   **1** Don't
         2 Don't
         3 Do
         4 Do
         5 Do
         6 Don't
         7 Don't
         8 Don't
A7   **A**
A8   biting
A9   **1** Yes
         2 Yes
         3 No
         4 Yes
         5 No
A10 engine, vehicle, sound, when

Answers to questions

Section 4

Turning left and right

A1   assess
       decide
       act

A2   **A**

A3   **B**

A4   Usually 2nd gear, but 1st if you need to go very slowly or 3rd if the corner is sweeping and you can take it safely at a higher speed

A5   **D**

Section 5

Emerging left and right

A1   two or more roads

A2   **A** T-junction
       B Y-junction
       C Roundabout
       D Staggered crossroads
       E Crossroads

A3   **1** E
       2 C
       3 B
       4 D
       5 A

A4   **A** 1
       B 3

A5   **1** Mirrors
       2 Signal
       3 Position
       4 Speed
       5 Look

A6   **1** mirrors, position
       2 signal
       3 safe
       4 safe distance
       5 overtake

A7   vision is limited

A8   **A** 2
       B 2

Section 6

Emergency stop

A1   **1** True
       2 True
       3 True
       4 False. Looking in the mirror should not be necessary. You should know what is behind you.
       5 False
       6 True
       7 True

A2   False. An emergency stop will be conducted randomly on only some tests. You must always know how to stop safely in an emergency.

A3   steer, brake
       1 False. Other elements beyond braking can cause skidding e.g. acceleration or going too fast into a bend.
       2 False. Although you may stop in a shorter distance, you still need to leave the correct distance to allow yourself time to react and vehicles behind you time to stop.

A4   double

A5   **1**

A6   very light

A7   False, because your tyres are not in contact with the road

A8   brakes

A9   **1** The driver
       2 The vehicle
       3 The road conditions

A10 **1** Slowing
       2 Speeding
       3 Turning
       4 Uphill, downhill

Section 7

MSM/PSL – hazard routine

A1   speed, behaviour, intentions

A2   Observe that the view into the new road is restricted. The driver should...
Move forward slowly, to get a better view.
Note the pedestrian who may walk in front of or behind car **A**.
Note the pedestrian waiting to cross.
Allow the cyclist to pass.
Once in position to see car **B**, stop and give way.

A3   Observe that the parked car restricts the view into and out of the side road. The driver should...
Slow down on approach to parked car **P**.
Take up position to gain a better view and be more visible to car **A** and the pedestrian.
Slow down in case the pedestrian walks out from behind the parked car **P**.
Consider signal to pass parked car **P**.
Look carefully into minor road. Note the actions of car **A**. Be prepared to stop.

A4   **1** Junctions
2 Hump-back bridges
3 Concealed entrances
4 Dead ground
5 Narrow lanes

A5   **1** Children playing
2 Horses
3 Pedestrians
4 Especially elderly and young cyclists
5 Other vehicles

A6   **1** True. The ability to advise those at your destination of delays can help to reduce the worry of late arrivals
2 True. This applies even if you're stopped at traffic lights or queueing in traffic
3 True
4 True
5 True
6 False

Section 8

Dealing with traffic

A1   necessary

A2   **1** Mirrors
2 Position
3 Speed
4 Look
5 Mirrors
6 Signal
7 Manoeuvre

A3   Vehicle 2

A4   Vehicle 2, even though the obstruction is on the right. Where safe, when travelling downhill be prepared to give priority to vehicles (especially heavy vehicles) that are coming uphill.

A5   **1, 4**

Section 9

Pedestrian and level crossings

A1   **1** True
2 True. You must not park or wait on the zig-zag lines on either side of the crossing.
3 False. You must not overtake on the zig-zag lines on approach to the crossing.
4 True
5 True. A slowing down arm signal should be used. It helps pedestrians understand what you intend to do. They cannot see your brake lights.

A2   **1** Traffic lights
2 Zig-zag lines
3 A white stop line

A3   **1** Flashing amber
2 You must give way to pedestrians on the crossing, but if it is clear you may go on.

A4   A bleeping tone. This sounds when the red light shows to drivers and helps visually impaired pedestrians know when it is safe to cross.

A5   There is no flashing amber light sequence. The light sequence is the same as normal traffic lights.

A6   cyclists

Answers to questions

A7   **A** 3
       B 1
       C 2
       D 4
A8   **2**
       4
       5

Section 10

Crossroads

A1   **A 3** Crossroads. Priority for traffic on the major road. Never assume other drivers will give you priority.
       B 1 Unmarked crossroads
       C 2 Crossroads with give way lines at the end of your road. Give way to traffic on the major road.

A2   **1** red
       2 red and amber
       3 green
       4 amber
       5 red

A3   **1** green
       2 red and amber
       3 amber
       4 red

A4   **2**

A5   **1** No. If your exit is blocked you should not enter a yellow box junction.
       2 No. If your exit is blocked you should not enter a yellow box junction.
       3 Yes

A6   **1** True
       2 False. Always consider whether it is safe. Are there dangers the other driver cannot see? Remember, flashing headlamps has the same meaning as sounding the horn. It is a warning: 'I am here!' Sometimes it is taken to mean: 'I am here and I am letting you pass.'

Section 11

Roundabouts

A1   **C**

A2   **1** Left
       2 Left
       3 Right. Remember to use the MSM routine before signalling left to turn off.

A3   Cyclists can stay in the left-hand lane while signalling right to carry on round so they may travel across your exit path.

A4   **1** Left
       2 Going ahead
       3 Right

A5   mirrors, signal, position, speed, look

A6   **2**

Section 12

Starting on a hill and at an angle

A1   **1** False. You should check your mirrors and blindspot before moving out. Keep alert for other traffic as you pull out and stop if necessary.
       2 True
       3 False. Move out slowly and carefully.
       4 True. The closer you are, the greater the angle.
       5 True. As you move out, you are likely to move on to the right-hand side of the road and into conflict with oncoming vehicles.
       6 False. You should signal only if it helps or warns other road users. Signalling gives you no right to pull out.

A2   **1** True
       2 False. Using the accelerator pedal will not move the car forwards.
       3 False. As your feet will be using the clutch pedal and the accelerator pedal you need to use the handbrake to stop the car rolling back.
       4 True
       5 True
       6 True
       7 True

Answers to questions

A3 **1** True
2 False. Almost certainly you will need to use the foot-brake.
3 False. It is often better to move off in 2nd gear.
4 True. This will stop the car rolling forwards.
5 True
6 False. You will need to have your foot on the foot-brake to stop the car rolling forwards.

A4 The following statements are correct: 1, 4, 5, 6, 7

Section 13

Other types of road

A1 **A** is the correct sign for a one-way street.
B tells you 'Ahead only'.
A2 **1** True
2 True
3 True
4 True
A3 **A** Dual carriageway ends
B Road narrows on both sides
C Two-way traffic straight ahead
A4 **A** and **C**
A5 **2** as statements 1, 3, 4 and 5 do not apply:
1 Reflective studs are used on some dual carriageways.
3 The speed limit is subject to local conditions and may vary from 40mph up to the national speed limit.
4 You can turn right on to and off dual carriageways unlike motorways, where all traffic enters and leaves on the left.
5 You may find slow moving vehicles sometimes displaying a flashing amber light.
A6 The speed limit applies to all lanes. Use the first lane to travel in and the second for overtaking.
A7 **A** You would cross over the first carriageway then wait in the gap in the central reservation. Be careful, if you are towing or if your vehicle is long, that you do not cause other road users to change course or slow down.
B You would wait until there is a gap in the traffic long enough for you safely to clear the first carriageway and emerge into the second.

A8 Traffic is moving much faster, and one or more lanes will have to be crossed.

Section 14

Reversing

A1 safe, convenient, law
A2 **1** False
2 False
3 True
4 True
A3 **A**
A4 **3**
A5 **1** True
2 False
3 True
A6 **4**
A7 **C**
A8 Left
A9 The front of the car will swing out to the right
A10 **1** True
2 False
3 True
A11 pedestrians, road users, stop
A12 True
A13 **2**
A14 **2**
A15 **B**

Section 15

Parking

A1 **2**
A2 **2**
A3 **C** in line with the rear of the parked vehicle
A4 **1** To the left
2 The nearside headlamp of the vehicle towards which you are reversing
3 Clipping the rear offside of the lead car
4 Take off the left lock
5 Steer to the right and then take off the right lock as you get straight
A5 **1** False
2 False
3 True. You will be expected to be able to complete the exercise within approximately two car lengths.
A6 All round, particularly for pedestrians and oncoming vehicles

Answers to questions

A7   **C** The other bay widths are reduced by parked vehicles. This may make opening doors a squeeze

A8   Allows you to make best use of the area in front of the bay. Gives you a better view when driving out of the space

A9   close, directions, pedestrians

A10   **1** False
       2 True
       3 True

A11   Answers might include to remove things from the boot, or when using a pushchair

A12   observe, pedestrians

A13   Any of the following:
at a bus stop
at a school entrance
opposite a junction
on a bend
on the brow of a hill
on a Clearway
on a motorway
at night facing oncoming traffic
in a residents' parking zone.

Section 16

Turning in the road

A1   **A**

A2   slowly, briskly

A3   False, but you should try to complete the manoeuvre in as few moves as possible.

A4   **2, 3, 4**

A5   all round

A6   **1** Right
       2 Steer briskly left
       3 Left
       4 Steer briskly right
       5 Right

A7   **1** Left
       2 Over your right shoulder to where the car is going

Section 17

Keeping space

A1   **C** well to the left but not too close to the kerb

A2   **B** Avoid swerving in and out. It is unnecessary and confuses other drivers.

A3   breaks, two-second

A4   **3**

A5   **1** safe
       2 considerate
       3 legal

A6   Cars 1, 2, 3, 6

A7   **1** False
       2 False
       3 True
       4 True
       5 False. Although not best practice, it's fine to park on the opposite side of the road as long as it's safe to do so.

Section 18

Use of speed

A1   **1** No
       2 Yes
       3 Yes
       4 No

A2   ½ second

A3   **1** 23 metres/75 feet
       2 15 metres/50 feet
       3 96 metres/315 feet

A4   longer, more

A5   speed, gear, position

A6   **1**

A7   **B**

A8   **A**

A9   **A** On a right-hand bend keep to the left. This will help to improve your view.
       B On a left-hand bend keep to the centre of the lane. Do not move to the centre of the road to get a better view. A vehicle travelling in the opposite direction may be taking the bend wide.

Section 19

Adverse weather conditions

A1   **2**

A2   Switch on earlier, switch off later.

A3   **1** It helps others to see you.

A4   **A** Always park with the flow of traffic. You will show red reflectors to vehicles travelling in your direction.

A5   In poor weather conditions – see and be seen

A6   dazzle, handbrake

A7   **4**

A8   double

A9   aquaplaning

A10 Slow down
Allow time for the tread patterns to
disperse the water.
A11 **2**
A12 very light
A13 **2**
A14 **1** Slow down
2 stop
3 windscreen wipers
4 demister, heated rear windscreen
A15 100 metres/328 feet
A16 **2**
A17 **2**
A18 **1** windows, audio system, Listen
2 early
3 brakes, alert
4 horn, warn
A19 brakes
A20 **1** gently
2 lower gear
3 drop, brakes
A21 **1**
A22 If possible, control your speed
before reaching the hill. Select
a low gear early.
A23 Using your brakes
A24 Avoid harsh acceleration
A25 **1** The driver
2 The vehicle
3 The road conditions
A26 **1** Slowing
2 Speeding
3 Turning
4 Uphill, downhill

Section 20

Vulnerable road users

A1 bike
A2 About the width of a small car, more in
windy or poor weather conditions
A3 **2** A white stick means the pedestrian is
visually impaired. A white stick with two
reflector bands means the pedestrian
may be deaf as well as visually impaired.
A4 **1** False
2 True
3 True
4 False. Pedestrians who are already
crossing have priority.
A5 Choose two from pedestrians, cyclists
or motorcyclists

Section 21

Vehicle checks

A1 1
A2 Oil
A3 3
A4 Water, anti-freeze, air
A5 1
A6 dazzle
A7 clean
A8 uneven, bulges, cuts
A9 2
A10 Get them checked as soon as possible
A11 **1** Neglect
2 routine checks
3 preventative
4 abuse

Section 22

Automatics

A1 Clutch
A2 **1** Driving is easier
2 There is more time to concentrate on
the road
A3 Park – Locks the transmission; select
only when the vehicle is stationary.
Reverse – Enables the car to go
backwards, as in a manual car.
Neutral – Has the same function as in a
manual car. The engine is not in contact
with the driving wheels.
Drive – Is used for driving forwards.
It automatically selects the most
appropriate gear.
3rd – Has the same function as
manual gears
2nd – Has the same function as
manual gears
1st – Has the same function as
manual gears
A4 3
A5 **1** Yes
2 No
3 Yes, if you needed extra control
4 You would probably use kickdown,
but in some circumstances you would
manually select a lower gear
5 Yes, maybe using 1st gear
6 No. Use the brakes
A6 **1** The right foot
2 The right foot

Answers to questions

A7 It stops you trying to control the brake and accelerator at the same time. It encourages early release of the accelerator and progressive braking.

A8 Drive, reverse, all forward gears.

A9 **1** Apply the handbrake every time you stop. Otherwise you have to keep your foot on the foot-brake.

A10 Park (P) or Neutral (N)

A11 **1**

Section 23

The test

A1 **1** False
2 True
3 False
4 False
5 True

A2 **3**

A3 Provisional licence

A4 **2**

A5 The test will not proceed. You have failed not only the eyesight section, but the whole test. Remember, if you wear glasses or contact lenses, to wear them for the eyesight test and for the rest of the driving test.

A6 False. You can make some less serious faults and still reach the required standard.

A7 False. If you did not hear clearly or did not understand what the examiner said, you should ask him or her to repeat the instruction. If you have any problem with your hearing, it is advisable to tell the examiner at the start of the test.

A8 **2** The examiner will expect you to drive normally. You should abide by all speed limits and drive according to road and traffic conditions.

A9 **1** Give you a verbal explanation of the main reasons for failure.
2 Write out a form for you to take away showing you your main errors.

A10 **1, 4**

A11 **1** Drive unsupervised
2 Drive without L plates

A12 No. You must have had at least three years' driving experience (and be over 21 years of age).

Section 24

After the test

A1 No

A2 Choose from bad weather driving, night-time driving, motorway driving and skid control, plus many others.

A3 **2**

A4 **1**

A5 **1** No
2 Yes, as long as the car has dual controls
3 Yes
4 No
5 Yes
6 Yes
7 Yes
8 No

A6 **3** You should never attempt to retrieve anything from the carriageway.

A7 **3**

A8 **3**

A9 **1** False
2 False
3 False
4 True
5 False

Part 4:
Glossary

Glossary

Accelerate

To make the vehicle move faster by pressing the right-hand pedal.

Advanced stop lines

A marked area on the road at traffic lights, which permits cyclists or buses to wait in front of other traffic.

Adverse weather

Bad weather that makes driving difficult or dangerous.

Alert

Quick to notice possible hazards.

Anticipation

Looking out for hazards and taking action before a problem starts.

Anti-lock brakes

Brakes that stop the wheels locking so that you are less likely to skid on a slippery road.

Aquaplane

To slide out of control on a wet road surface.

Articulated vehicle

A long vehicle that is divided into two or more sections joined by cables.

Attitude

The way you think or feel, which affects the way you drive. Especially, whether you are patient and polite, or impatient and aggressive.

Automatic

A vehicle with gears that change by themselves as you speed up or slow down.

Awareness

Taking notice of the road and traffic conditions around you at all times.

Black ice

An invisible film of ice that forms over the road surface, creating very dangerous driving conditions.

Blind spot

The section of road behind you that you cannot see in your mirrors. You 'cover' your blind spot by looking over your shoulder before moving off or overtaking.

Brake fade

Loss of power to the brakes when you have been using them for a long time without taking your foot off the brake pedal. For example, when driving down a steep hill. The brakes will overheat and not work properly.

Braking distance

The distance you must allow to slow the vehicle in order to come to a stop.

Brow

The highest point of a hill.

Built-up area

A town, or place with lots of buildings.

Carriageway

One side of a road or motorway. A 'dual carriageway' has a central reservation.

Catalytic converter

A piece of equipment fitted in the exhaust system that changes harmful gases into less harmful ones.

Chicane

A sharp double bend that has been put into a road to make traffic slow down.

Child restraint

A child seat or special seat belt for children. It keeps them safe and stops them moving around in the car.

Clearway

A road where no stopping is allowed at any time. The sign for a clearway is a red cross in a red circle on a blue background.

Coasting
Driving a vehicle without using any of the gears. That is, with your foot on the clutch pedal and the car in neutral.

Commentary driving
Talking to yourself about what you see on the road ahead and what action you are going to take – an aid to concentration.

Comprehensive insurance
A motor insurance policy that pays for all repairs even if you cause an accident.

Concentration
Keeping all your attention on your driving.

Conditions
How good or bad the road surface is, volume of traffic on the road, and what the weather is like.

Congestion
Heavy traffic that makes it difficult to get to where you want to go.

Consideration
Thinking about other road users and not just yourself. For example, letting another driver go first at a junction.

Contraflow
When traffic on a motorway follows signs to move to the opposite carriageway for a short distance because of roadworks. (During a contraflow, there is traffic driving in both directions on the same side of the motorway.)

Coolant
Liquid in the radiator that removes heat from the engine.

Defensive driving
Driving safely without taking risks, looking out for hazards and thinking for others.

Disqualified
Stopped from doing something (eg driving) by law, because you have broken the law.

Distraction
Anything that stops you concentrating on your driving, such as talking to passengers or using your mobile phone.

Document
An official paper or card, eg your driving licence.

Dual carriageway
A road or motorway with a central reservation.

Engine braking – *see also* gears
Using the low gears to keep your speed down. For example, when you are driving down a steep hill and you want to stop the vehicle running away. Using the gears instead of braking will help to prevent brake fade.

Environment
The world around us and the air we breathe.

Equestrian crossing
An unusual kind of crossing. It has a button high up for horse riders to push.

Exceed
Go higher than an upper limit.

Exhaust emissions
Gases that come out of the exhaust pipe to form part of the outside air.

Field of vision
How far you can see in front and around you when you are driving.

Filler cap
Provides access to the vehicle's fuel tank, for filling up with petrol or diesel.

Glossary

Fog lights

Extra bright rear (and sometimes front) lights that may be used in very poor visibility due to fog. You must remember to switch them off when visibility improves, as they can dazzle and distract other drivers.

Ford

A place in a stream or river that is shallow enough to drive across with care.

Four-wheel drive (4WD)

On a conventional vehicle, steering and engine speed affect just two 'drive' wheels. On 4WD, they affect all four wheels, ensuring optimum grip on loose ground.

Frustration

Feeling annoyed because you cannot drive as fast as you want to because of other drivers or heavy traffic.

Fuel consumption

The amount of fuel (petrol or diesel) that your vehicle uses. Different vehicles have different rates of consumption. Increased fuel consumption means using more fuel. Decreased fuel consumption means using less fuel.

Fuel gauge

A display or dial on the instrument panel that tells you how much fuel (petrol or diesel) you have left.

Gantry

An overhead platform like a high narrow bridge that displays electric signs on a motorway.

Gears

Control the speed of the engine in relation to the vehicle's speed. May be hand operated (manual) or automatically controlled. In a low gear (such as first or second), the engine runs more slowly. In a high gear (such as fourth or fifth), it runs more quickly. Putting the car into a lower gear as you drive can create the effect of engine braking – forcing the engine to run more slowly.

Handling

How well your vehicle moves or responds when you steer or brake.

Harass

To drive in a way that makes other road users afraid.

Hard shoulder

The single lane to the left of the inside lane on a motorway, which is for emergency use only. You should not drive on the hard shoulder except in an emergency, or when there are signs telling you to use the hard shoulder because of roadworks.

Harsh braking (or harsh acceleration)

Using the brake (or accelerator) too hard so as to cause wear on the engine.

Hazard warning lights

Flashing amber lights that you should use only when you have broken down. On a motorway, you can use them to warn other drivers behind you of a hazard ahead.

High-sided vehicle

A van or truck with tall sides, or a tall trailer such as a caravan or horse-box, that is at risk of being blown off-course in strong winds.

Impatient
Not wanting to wait for pedestrians and other road users.

Inflate
To blow up – to put air in your tyres until they are at the right pressures.

Instrument panel
The car's electrical controls and gauges, set behind the steering wheel. Also called the dashboard.

Intimidate
To make someone feel afraid.

Involved
Being part of something. For example, being one of the drivers in an accident.

Jump leads
A pair of thick electric cables with clips at either end. You use it to charge a flat battery by connecting it to the live battery in another vehicle.

Junction
A place where two or more roads join.

Liability
Being legally responsible.

Manoeuvre
Using the controls to make your car move in a particular direction. For example, when turning, reversing or parking.

Manual
By hand. In a car that is a 'manual' or has manual gears, you have to change the gears yourself.

Maximum
The largest possible; 'maximum speed' is the highest speed allowed.

Minimum
The smallest possible.

Mirrors
Cars have a minimum of three rear view mirrors: one in the centre of the windscreen, and one on each front door. Additional mirrors may be required on longer vehicles, or when towing a high trailer such as a caravan. Some mirrors may be curved (convex or concave) to increase the field of vision. The mirror on the windscreen can be turned to anti-dazzle position, if glare from headlights behind creates a distraction.

Mobility
The ability to move around easily.

Monotonous
Boring. For example, a long stretch of motorway with no variety and nothing interesting to see.

MOT
The test that proves your car is safe to drive. Your MOT certificate is one of the important documents for your vehicle.

Motorway
A fast road that has two or more lanes on each side and a hard shoulder. Drivers must join or leave it on the left, via a motorway junction. Many kinds of slower vehicles – such as bicycles – are not allowed on motorways.

Multiple-choice questions
Questions with several possible answers where you have to try to choose the right one.

Observation
The ability to notice important information, such as hazards developing ahead.

Obstruct
To get in the way of another road user.

Octagonal
Having eight sides.

Glossary

Oil level

The amount of oil needed for the engine to run effectively. The oil level should be checked as part of your regular maintenance routine, and the oil replaced as necessary.

Pedestrian

A person walking.

Pelican crossing

A crossing with traffic lights that pedestrians can use by pushing a button. Cars must give way to pedestrians on the crossing while the amber light is flashing. You must give pedestrians enough time to get to the other side of the road.

Perception

Seeing or noticing (as in Hazard Perception).

Peripheral vision

The area around the edges of your field of vision.

Positive attitude

Being sensible and obeying the law when you drive.

Priority

The vehicle or other road user that is allowed by law to go first is the one that has priority.

Provisional licence

A first driving licence. All learner drivers must get one before they start having lessons.

Puffin crossing

A type of pedestrian crossing that does not have a flashing amber light phase.

Reaction time

The amount of time it takes you to see a hazard and decide what to do about it.

Red route

You see these in London and some other cities. Double red lines at the edge of the road tell you that you must not stop or park there at any time. Single red lines have notices with times when you must not stop or park. Some red routes have marked bays for either parking or loading at certain times.

Red warning triangle

An item of safety equipment to carry in your car in case you break down. You can place the triangle 45m behind your car on the same side of the road. It warns traffic that your vehicle is causing an obstruction. (Do not use these on motorways.)

Residential areas

Areas of housing where people live. The speed limit is 30mph or sometimes 20mph.

Road hump

A low bump built across the road to slow vehicles down. Also called 'sleeping policemen'.

Rumble strips

Raised strips across the road near a roundabout or junction that change the sound the tyres make on the road surface, warning drivers to slow down. They are also used on motorways to separate the main carriageway from the hard shoulder.

Safety margin

The amount of space you need to leave between your vehicle and the one in front so that you are not in danger of crashing into it if the driver slows down suddenly or stops. Safety margins have to be longer in wet or icy conditions.

Separation distance

The amount of space you need to leave between your vehicle and the one in front so that you are not in danger of crashing into it if the driver slows down suddenly or stops. The separation distance must be longer in wet or icy conditions.

Security coded radio

To deter thieves, a radio or CD unit that requires a security code (or pin number) to operate it.

Single carriageway

Generally, a road with one lane in each direction.

Skid

When the tyres fail to grip the surface of the road, the subsequent loss of control of the vehicle's movement is called a skid. Usually caused by harsh or fierce braking, steering or acceleration.

Snaking

Moving from side to side. This sometimes happens with caravans or trailers when you drive too fast, or they are not properly loaded.

Staggered junction

Where you drive cross another road. Instead of going straight across, you have to go a bit to the right or left.

Steering

Control of the direction of the vehicle. May be affected by road surface conditions: when the steering wheel turns very easily, steering is 'light', and when you have to pull hard on the wheel it is described as 'heavy'.

Sterile

Clean and free from bacteria.

Stopping distance

The time it takes for you to stop your vehicle – made up of 'thinking distance' and 'braking distance'.

Supervisor

Someone who sits in the passenger seat with a learner driver. They must be over 21 and have held a full driving licence for at least three years.

Tailgating

Driving too closely behind another vehicle – usually to harass the driver in front.

Thinking distance

The time it takes you to notice something and take the right action. You need to add thinking distance to your braking distance to make up your total stopping distance.

Third party insurance

An insurance policy that insures you against any claim by passengers or other persons for damage or injury to their person or property.

Toucan crossing

A type of pedestrian crossing that does not have a flashing amber light phase, and cyclists are allowed to ride across.

Tow

To pull something behind your vehicle. It could be a caravan or trailer.

Traffic-calming measures

Speed humps, chicanes and other devices placed in roads to slow traffic down.

Tram

A public transport vehicle that moves along the streets on fixed rails, usually electrically powered by overhead lines.

Tread depth

The depth of the grooves in a car's tyres that help them grip the road surface. The grooves must all be at least 1.6mm deep.

Glossary

Turbulence

Strong movement of air. For example, when a large vehicle passes a much smaller one.

Two-second rule

In normal driving, the ideal minimum distance between you and the vehicle in front can be timed using the 'two-second' rule. As the vehicle in front passes a fixed object (such as a signpost), say to yourself 'Only a fool breaks the two second rule'. It takes two seconds to say it. If you have passed the same object before you finish, you are too close – pull back.

Tyre pressures

The amount of air that must be pumped into a tyre in order for it to be correctly blown up.

Vehicle Excise Duty

The tax you pay for your vehicle so that you may drive it on public roads, also known as road tax.

Vehicle Registration Certificate

A record of details about a vehicle and its owner, also known as a log book.

Vehicle watch scheme

A system for identifying vehicles that may have been stolen.

Vulnerable

At risk of harm or injury.

Waiting restrictions

Times when you may not park or load your vehicle in a particular area.

Wheel balancing

To ensure smooth rotation at all speeds, wheels need to be 'balanced' correctly. This is a procedure done at a garage or tyre centre, when each wheel is removed for testing. Balancing may involve minor adjustment with the addition of small weights, to avoid wheel wobble.

Wheel-spin

When the vehicle's wheels spin round out of control with no grip on the road surface.

Zebra crossing

A pedestrian crossing without traffic lights. It has an orange light, and is marked by black and white stripes on the road. Drivers must stop for pedestrians to cross.